UNLOCK THE POWER WITHIN
A JOURNEY TO SELF-DISCOVERY AND EMPOWERMENT

By
Michelle Marriott

Copyright © 2025 by Michelle Marriott

ALL RIGHTS RESERVED

Grow, my lovely.

Heal your wounds

Feel your heart

Feel it bloom

Embrace the darkness

Let it emerge with your light

You have the courage,

And the strength to fight

As transformation

Occurs inside

To be your authentic self

With no need to hide

I know that path

Left you in a spin

It won't be long,

For happiness to begin

Be patient,

The Suffering will end.

It's when darkness comes

Your forever friend

Michelle Marriott

Acknowledgement

I would like to say a huge thank you to Amanda Thomas, a dear friend of mine. Throughout my spiritual journey, she has supported me and been my rock through my darkest days. Amanda is one of the earth angels, as I call them. Her words are inspiring and encouraging and often hold messages. Not only has she supported me through my spiritual journey, but she has also supported me on my writing journey. I will forever be grateful for a truly amazing friend.

I would also like to thank my two daughters, Cara and Melissa, and my two sons, Corey and Jaiden, who have all supported me on my spiritual path without judgment. I'm so lucky to have such wonderful children.

I would like to thank Jaiden for his expertise in technology, which made this book possible.

In memory of

I would also like to thank my nana, Pearl Dennis, for your support from the other side. My nana was my guardian angel during my times of despair and continues to be my guardian angel today. She often visited me during my dreams, guiding me out of a dark place and sending me messages and guidance.

Hi, Nana. I am so sorry I complained about your cigarette smoke; it is that which lets me know you're around. I did it, you know; I broke those generational curses. You were right; I believed you even when the doctors didn't. I know you are smiling because I can see and feel you. You are proud of me. As the tears of joy fall down my face, my heart fills with so much love; I hold you close, and that is where you will stay. Thank you for being by my side.

I love you always, Shelley.

I would also like to thank Landon Maiden for supporting me on my path from the spirit realm.

Landon, I saw your soul before your human form, the moment I met you. You are a passionate, loving, caring, intelligent, wise soul that continues to shine even in the spirit realm. I know you fought battles and demons in your waking life, and I wish I could have done more, but I understand that I was fighting battles and demons, too, and I did the best I could with the knowledge I had at the time. I feel your presence often, and I see you riding your KTM bike. I know you visit my dreams, and I am so grateful for the support and messages you send me on my spiritual journey. I am so blessed that we crossed paths, and I will never forget you. I will see you in my next dream.

All my love, Shelley.

I also want to thank my brother Carl Bee, who is also on the other side, for my lovely message.

I have not forgotten you, bro. I know you, too, also had your inner demons and battles to deal with, and you tried so hard; I could see that. Sometimes I still play your song, and I know you too have visited me, giving me messages, but at the time, I was so ignorant, wasn't I? I didn't trust in my gifts to notice your messages, and for that, I'm truly sorry. It must have taken some real effort to send those messages when I was in a low vibration. Well, now I'm in high vibration, so it won't be so hard. Anyway, thank you for your support and guiding me on my spiritual journey.

I miss and love your loads. Shelley.

TABLE OF CONTENTS

Introduction 1
The Awakening 5
What is a spiritual awakening? 15
Moving past the loop 43
Into the subconscious mind via dreams 51
What is shadow work, and why is it important for spiritual growth?
.... 57
The wounded inner child 63
Give up the search, you're looking in the wrong places. 73
What is grounding? 77
Why journaling is a powerful tool 79
Practicing self-love 86
The ego 92
Ancestral healing 95
The importance of setting boundaries 99
Rewiring the brain 101
The forgotten chakras 110
The power of crystals 115
Understanding the masculine and feminine energies 118
The self-discovery path 122
Chasing dopamine's 125

We all have psychic abilities 128
The art of manifestation 132
Angel numbers 143
Understanding synchronicities 145
What does it mean to surrender? 151
When the universe steps in 159
The intelligence of the human body 171
Conscious living 175
About The Author 199
Book recommendations 200

In search of happiness

Take with you your eyes

In search for love

Take with you your heart

In search for peace

Take with you your ears

But it is only in the stillness of your mind

That you will find them all

Introduction

Did you know we are born with the knowledge and wisdom already within us?

Yes, that's right! You don't need external sources like the internet, just your own inner compass! All you must do is remove the baggage that you have been accumulating throughout life that is blocking you from accessing this sacred knowledge, and in this book, I will guide you on how to do just that.

In this book, I will help you understand the belief system and how it can hijack your brain and stop you from manifesting your goals and dreams by helping you recognize the stories you tell yourself that are not necessarily true, giving you more clarity and self-awareness to understand yourself on a much deeper level.

I will also guide you on how you can rewire your brain into thinking more positively and free yourself from the limitations holding you back.

What if I told you that there is infinite access to a higher power guiding you on your journey? That power is your higher self; you are the universe!! The creator of your own reality, and you can connect to that higher power at any given time. How amazing would that be?

Once you begin to know yourself on a deeper level, you begin to ignite your intuition and awaken the power within!! This allows you to open doors to the infinite possibilities. Your intuition will guide you as you receive insight, which will help you navigate through life as well as help you make better decisions in reaching your goals and dreams.

I have always been able to tap into my psychic abilities ever since I was a little girl. We are all born with psychic abilities, but we suppress them due to the social environment and our upbringing.

It all starts with igniting your intuition, and with self-love, compassion, consistency, patience, and action, you will soon be on your way to tapping into yours. Of course, it involves lots of hard work, and you will go through many challenges on the way, but I promise that if you put in the effort and work, you will be heading for a more peaceful, happy, and fulfilling life that will just flow effortlessly!

You will be diving deep into your shadows and pulling out some emotional baggage, but remember, there are also gifts and talents hidden in the shadows that you may discover on the way. Although some parts are going to be uncomfortable to start with, there will also be some amazing experiences, and it's those amazing experiences that make the challenging parts seem less challenging, and in time, those challenges will be much easier to overcome.

There will always be challenges in your life, but once the inner work is being done, new insight and a different perspective will surface, making challenges feel less challenging. When you live more intuitively, you become the ultimate creator of your own reality; you flow with life with less stress, allowing you to manifest your goals and dreams much quicker. It will take time and patience, but the outcome is so rewarding and empowering.

This book will offer guidance, but it's up to you to put in the work and discover the magic waiting for you.

When you connect more deeply with yourself, you discover your guides and angels, and you start to connect with them. You realize that everything is connected and that you are the god within. This gives you a sense of security, knowing that you are not alone and you are blessed every step of the way.

In this book, I will share with you my personal experiences on how I came from a dark place into the light and how I tapped into my inner power to create the life I've always wanted.

I will share with you some of the tools that I used to overcome depression and anxiety, and how I discovered my true purpose.

My name is Michelle, and my purpose is to share my knowledge and the experiences that have shaped me into who I am today. Turning pain into power! My mission is to pass that knowledge on to others who are struggling in life and have lost their way, giving them the tools needed to live a happier, peaceful, fulfilling life. Not only that, but I will guide you on a path to help you heal the mind, body, and soul.

Ok, it's going to take some hard work and determination on your part, but if you are reading this book, I know you're halfway there; although it doesn't seem like it at this moment, it's all upwards from here!

So, are you ready for the most empowering journey of your life and say goodbye to the fear, stress and anxieties that were holding you back and say hello to a more calming and peaceful life? Because if you are not ready, then put this book down and go back to it when you're ready and trust me, you will know when you are ready!

Throughout this book, you will see a series of poetry and quotes that I wrote on my healing journey, some of which come from when I was in a dark place and some from a light place. I write on my days when I'm down; I call this soul searching. I hope that my words will spark inspiration in you.

You must take the good with the bad, and writing helps me through the tough days, and that is my healthy coping mechanism. You might find painting, dancing, or other ways as your coping mechanism, but eventually, your darkest days won't seem so bad as your shadows hold some profound creativity in there amongst the forgotten parts.

It was reading other people's spiritual awakening experiences that got me through mine, and I hope that this book will help you, too. I wish you all the love and light on your journey to peace and happiness.

The Awakening

For over 45 years, I suffered from depression due to a significant amount of sexual abuse and trauma from a young age. I grew up thinking it was normal for a dad to watch pornographic movies in front of his daughter. I eventually realized that this was a form of brainwashing. I don't want to go too much into the abuse, as that's not what this book is about, but it gives you an idea of how I came from a dark place and into the light.

By the time I was 21, I was diagnosed with what they called an emotionally unstable borderline personality disorder that eventually escalated into a rare type of bipolar called rapid cycling bipolar disorder. I was medicated for it and had been placed on many different types of medication.

I was also prescribed diazepam to calm me down, as I would often rock uncontrollably and pull out my hair while scratching my body. This was because I wasn't dealing with my emotions in a healthy way and had no idea how to handle them.

For the duration of 30 years, I had different types of counselling, but nothing worked. The truth is, I was looking for someone outside of myself to fix my problems as though someone had a magic wand that could miraculously make them disappear, and because I didn't hear the results I wanted to hear, the rest went over my head. Plus, doing the inner work was not only difficult to keep on top of when you suffer from depression, but it was also time-consuming when you have children to deal with, or at least that is what I had thrown into my belief system.

The medication they prescribed wasn't working; in fact, it was pointless trying to live a life as most days; the medication left me emotionless and numb. I was like a walking zombie.

I was stuck in what I call a loop. A rollercoaster of emotions that I didn't understand. One minute, I felt happy, and the next, I was having suicidal thoughts. I didn't know how to deal with my emotions. Each time I tried to pick myself up, I was knocked back down. Often spent days, even months, crying in bed, and each time I always ended up thinking about my past and all the things that happened to me. No matter how hard I tried, I could not get out of that cycle.

I didn't understand that the reason we go back into our past, into our shadows, is because it wants us to understand what happened; it wants us to feel the emotion to make sense of it so we can let it go, but instead, I thought by ignoring it and moving on was a sign of strength and oh boy! Was I wrong?

My life took a turn for the worst when I reached the age of 23; that was the age I took the first overdose. I remember thinking that I just did not want to live anymore, as there was no meaning to my existence. It was touch-and-go on whether I would pull through it. The doctors told my parents to be prepared for the worst because if I did survive, there would be a significant amount of brain damage. I guess the universe had other plans for me.

The words I often heard from my dad were that the way to a man's heart was through sex, so when I met someone for the first time, that's exactly what I did, as I thought that's how I would receive love in return.

I didn't know that the love you seek is within yourself and not outside of yourself, but how could I love someone like me? How could I love someone who hurts their children by allowing them to see self-harming acts? How can I love someone who feels ashamed of herself for watching porn in front of her dad? How can I love someone who jumps into bed with someone in desperate need of love? These were the thoughts in my head that I had to keep quiet all my life because I was ashamed of myself and embarrassed to tell anyone.

I wasn't taught to love myself; I wasn't taught boundaries; I wasn't shown love. I wasn't taught how to respect myself. I was just taught that sex sells; sex is what gets you love, and sex is what gets you money. The number of times I was used by a guy while seeking love was horrendous.

The ironic thing about my dad is that he often played a good dad; underneath his perverted ways, he still took on a good father role. He could also give good advice, like when he told me to look in a mirror and tell myself that I was beautiful. I knew that this was just a way of building my confidence up, ready for what he had in store for me, which you will see further in this book.

I always knew that with a little makeup, I looked beautiful on the outside, but somewhere deep down, I didn't want to be just eye candy; there was more to me than that. I wanted to be soul food.

I was over the moon with joy when I first found out that I got into college to do a psychology course, only to have my dreams shattered by my dad's words. He told me I wasn't clever enough to do psychology and laughed in my face! It's sex that sells, he replied. It was as though Intelligence was forbidden in our house.

I didn't even take any exams at school because of my dad's words, so I lived my life believing I couldn't do any other jobs apart from cleaning jobs because I was never going to sell my body; that was most definitely taken off my list of jobs.

I met my first abusive partner when I was just 19. He was physically abusive and mentally abusive, and truth be known, he used me for the whole 6 years. He wanted somewhere to stay, and I had a home to provide for him. From then on, the abusive partners just continued. It became a repeated pattern for several years. In fact, dating good guys did not feel right.

I eventually had four beautiful children and always did my best for them. A lot of my depression they never saw; they just thought I was ill because I didn't want to expose those parts of me to my children. In time, you develop coping mechanisms that allow you to just shut off the suffering, but you become so numb to everything else, including the beauty in life. But this only shows up in your body, which I had to find out on my awakening journey. So, if I wasn't depressed, I was physically ill. It becomes a crippling disease in the end, both mentally and physically.

I remember thinking about my children, and they should not have to see me in this state. I tried to hide it as much as I could, so when I cried, it was often done in silence by myself. Each time I took an overdose, it was out of shame because what mother would allow their children to see such a thing? My children deserve a good mum. Those were the sort of words I would speak to myself.

I tried so hard to help myself that I even took up CBT therapy and used it on myself. I often used to write my thoughts and feelings down to try and make sense of my emotions, but the pain was too difficult to take. I just wasn't ready to unleash and face the shadows.

It was difficult for me to be consistent with my mental health appointments, as some days, I could not get out of bed. I managed to get my children to school and give them supper, but then I was back in bed. So, it was hit and miss with my appointments, plus I was never honest with my past, but this was because so much got buried. The parts that were surfacing were the physical parts that were manifesting into illnesses such as tummy aches, migraines, incontinence problems, and muscular and joint pain. I had many trips to the doctors for arthritis, appendix, and brain tumors because of the number of headaches. It didn't occur to me that it was due to mental pain.

I was 38 years old when the penny finally dropped, and after a conversation with my friend, I let out a few things that had been happening to me, and that is when she said to me, "Shelley, this is sexual abuse; you have been abused all your life" I knew this as soon as she said it and it was though I had woke up from a dream!! It all came rushing back to me as though I was brainwashed!! But it still took an awful lot of counseling for it to sink in. I could not comprehend what had happened to me. I thought it was just the way he was; I thought it was just his personality.

I spent the next 3 months at my daughter's house, where I suffered a huge nervous breakdown. I spent that time sitting up in the spare room, trying to figure it all out. There is so much more to this story, but that's for another book, as I don't want to fill this book with my abusive upbringing, as that's not what this book is about. Instead, I just wanted to give you snippets so you can understand how I came from the dark to the light.

I didn't see my parents after that and eventually moved home.

They say that everything happens for a reason, including the bad stuff, and it's all for your higher good. If I hadn't witnessed the light, I would have laughed at that statement! But believe me when I say it's a true saying. You will understand more further in this book, but for now, I would like to invite you to be open-minded to all possibilities because it's important for healing and growth.

I started my spiritual awakening at the time when the global pandemic struck. I had moved to a more rural area in Lincolnshire at the time and lived on my own with my youngest son.

I hit a severe depressive state, and again, I started thinking about my past and all the dreadful things that had happened to me. Only this time, I had had enough! I broke down to my knees, and I stopped dwelling on my suffering. I don't want to end my life and refuse to be in victim mode. Instead, I got fiery, powerful, and angry! I stood up, and I said NO! I'm not doing it; I refuse to go down that route again. I said it with such power, with a fierce voice as though I had become this higher power! I stood up, and instantly, I felt the shift! As though, for the first time in my life, someone is listening to me.

I had no idea how I was going to do it, but I remember asking all these questions, like "What do I do from here?" "Where do I start?" Somehow, I knew that I would figure it out.

I started to see little quotes on Facebook as though they were messages for me. People and groups appeared from nowhere as if they were specifically for me. I started to follow these signs, and I started very small. The first thing I saw was clearing Facebook of negativity and switching off the news. That was a huge starting point for me. Before I knew it, my Facebook had only positive, empowering words and people on there.

It was as though my prayers had been answered. I started to feel less lonely, as though I wasn't alone anymore. I felt like I was being guided to my next move.

I got up one morning, and everything looked brighter! My senses were heightened, I could smell better, my vision was sharp, and my hearing was fantastic! It was as though I could see for the first time, as though I had woken up from a long dream. That was literally an awakening for me. I felt fantastic! I am with the beauty around me as though I were seeing the world for the first time.

Of course, it was short-lived, well, I say short-lived, but to be honest, that feeling comes and goes, but I never went back to the suffering. Instead, the darkness was somewhat different. Of course, it was uncomfortable, but this time, it taught me things. I saw it in a different light and from a new perspective.

I spent many sleepless nights, but I was flitting from moments of pure bliss to moments of sadness. In those moments of sadness, I found so much about myself, and the hidden gifts buried deep inside them.

I was guided to spiritual groups that spoke a lot about the dark night of the soul, and I started to research how to overcome trauma. In time, my memories started to flood back to me, some of which I didn't even know about; I had buried them so deeply. Instead of crying and ignoring them, I started to ask myself questions in my journal so I could make sense of them.

People would randomly text me saying things like, "Make sense of your memory, feel the emotion, then let go." These people I call messengers, as they pop into your life to give the message and then move on. They become so obvious in the end. At first, you ponder why they popped up out of the blue with a random message that leaves you scratching your head! I bet you can already recall a moment like that at some point in your life.

This is what I wrote about for a year in my journal, my memories, and as I did, I could feel them slipping away as though they had literally left my body, as though they had been stored there for years.

As time went on, it was easier to deal with them, and I felt much lighter for it. Sure, it was painful, but it was as though each time I did a bit of shadow work, I was rewarded with bliss! And that bliss felt good! As though I were in heaven, that is the only way I can describe it. When the bliss came, it made each shadow work feel like a walk in the park.

It wasn't all a bed of roses, and I had so much to heal and learn on my journey, but I was more determined than ever, and that was the important thing to me; that was my focus at the time. No matter what, I promised myself that I would deal with it and keep moving forward, and that I did.

Leaving the outside noise and going within to become a hermit was the best thing I ever did. I learnt from a young age to just smile and stay strong, and no one would suspect a thing. I was ignoring my emotions, and they were just piling up, and the number I became. Being raised with damaged parents left me in victim mode my entire life, and that victim mode just followed me everywhere I went. I once read a saying that said you have two choices: you can be the patient, or you can be the doctor. Don't you just love the power of words?

Her last words

I walk down a long, dark, Gitty
To find myself in a lonely city
I couldn't see for the mist and fog
Not a sound
Nor a bark from a dog

And so, I wait
In the hope of being found
In this dreadful silence
As I stare at the ground

Minutes and hours passed me by
All I could think to myself was, why
The Gitty had gone
There was no way out
Why was this
What's it about

I felt confused
Angry and sad
What had I done
That was so bad

A figure appeared

Where the Gitty was

I squinted my eye

And I looked through the fog

There she was

Waving her hand

As she whispered

In my ear

I understand.

In loving memory of Pearl Dennis.

What is a spiritual awakening?

A spiritual awakening is a profound experience that shifts your perception of the world around you and gives you a greater awareness of yourself and the world around you, making you want to go deeper into your inner world. It makes you question reality and who you are on a much deeper level. It's as though you have woken up from amnesia or a deep sleep. It shakes you to your very core to question your very existence. You start to feel connected to something much bigger than yourself.

It's about coming back to yourself before the world gets its hands on you. It's an awareness of a new reality. You feel called to uncover true meanings and the purpose of life. You may feel a calling to help others, or you may just want to heal yourself first. Once you awake, there is no going back.

Experiences like trauma, pandemics, twin flames, death, depression, divorce, and deep meditation can trigger a spiritual awakening, although some can wake without any of these triggers. A lot of children born today are already awake.

What Happens During a Spiritual Awakening

During a spiritual awakening, you can go through several experiences and challenges. Some days, you will feel so much joy, and on another day, you can feel sad for no reason. You can go through what is called an emotional rollercoaster. This is normal as your mind and body are adjusting to the new you.

Many things in your life can change, like your belief system and your values. You may suddenly change your career or want to make changes to your health, leading you to make healthy lifestyle choices. It can take time to integrate these changes into your life, so it's important to remain patient with yourself as you go through these transformations.

For me, I went through a healing process to heal my past, and then I went into healing my ancestors. This, in turn, broke generational patterns of unhealthy habits. These had to be dealt with before I could move to the next level on my journey, plus that's what I was guided to do.

Most people who are spiritually awake go through the dark night of the soul, which I will go into later, but not everyone goes through this, as it depends on many factors, like how your upbringing was.

I then started to understand the ego, and I learnt to see the ego for what it was (more about the ego later in this book). I started to recognise that we are all connected and that there are no separations.

I could see and feel energies, and I knew that something bigger than myself was at play. My consciousness started to expand into higher levels, and I was tapping into gifts and talents I never knew I had. It is amazing what we are capable of when we remove the baggage that we have accumulated throughout life.

I'm not going to sugarcoat it because the first year was a tough ride for me, and often, most people say the same thing because our minds and bodies must level up and release what no longer serves us. It's a new, profound reality that we are experiencing. In time, though, it's an amazing journey to be on, and amazing things start to happen. You feel blessed for the opportunity of an awakening.

My advice is to get yourself in groups with like-minded people because if you cannot understand or comprehend what is happening to you, then it can make you feel like you're going crazy! And believe me, this only leads to manifesting illnesses you don't want. The more support you have, the better.

Being in the groups will give you a better understanding of what is happening, and you won't feel alone on your spiritual path. You will realize that lots of others go through similar experiences, and this gives you a sense of relief.

Most likely, you will find yourself becoming a researcher. I know I did; I was obsessed with learning about it all, and I wanted to know more. I read many books that helped me on my path, and once you tap into your own inner power, you realize that the answers to your questions are already within you. Don't get me wrong, I still like to read good books.

What Does a Spiritual Awakening Feel Like

In the beginning, it feels like you're going insane! You feel like you're developing schizophrenia or other mental disorders. This is because we are all gifted with psychic abilities, so your gifts are advancing. You are waking up to the real, authentic you. Your abilities to create the life you want. You're becoming more sensitive to other people's energies, and it can take a while to adjust to those energies. It all feels weird because our ego brains cannot make sense of it because it doesn't fit into our box of what we have been taught about spirituality. It's always good to be open-minded and be prepared to unlearn what you have been taught and what you once believed to be true.

You may also experience hearing voices from the spirit realm or from spirit guides, but don't be alarmed by this because it's a normal part of the process. Not everyone will experience this, as it really depends on your unique gifts. I started hearing outside voices, but now my spirit guides are within me.

Be prepared to lose friends as your vibration rises and it no longer matches their low vibration. Although you may still speak to them, you find that you cannot tolerate their low vibrational energy because you become sensitive to it. Unless they are vibrating with you, we cannot take them with us on our journey. Most often, it's because they have finished what they came into your life to do, and that could be sitting with you in the darkness or helping you learn a lesson. Once the mission is fulfilled, they slip away from your life. Awakening for them will happen when they are ready. We are all on our own path; some are healing, some are learning lessons, and some are evolving, but as always, there's nothing wrong with planting the seed to help wake them up.

You start to feel more grounded and gain more clarity. You have a deeper sense of purpose and more self-awareness, and you feel connected with the world around you, including the universe/higher self. You have a new, profound, higher perspective on life.

There are some physical symptoms you may experience while going through a spiritual awakening, but this will level out in time. It is because it takes time for the body to catch up with the higher self/soul, and you're a spiritual being living a human experience.

Some of the physical symptoms you can experience are

1. Headaches
2. Palpitations
3. Sleep disturbance
4. Lightheadedness
5. Unexplained aches and pain
6. Night sweats
7. Changes in body temperature
8. Hot flushes
9. Weight loss
10. Emotional symptoms
11. Depression
12. Anxiety
13. Agitation
14. Irritable
15. Changing interest
16. Feeling alone
17. Hopelessness
18. Other symptoms
19. Heightened sensitivity to your surroundings
20. Heightened intuition
21. A sense of inner freedom

22. An intense sense of empathy and compassion for others

You may only experience some of these on the list, not necessarily experience all of them, and it's always a good idea to check symptoms with a doctor, as not everything is always spiritual, just as everything isn't always mundane.

Be Careful not to attach to any illness because we manifest all the time, whether it's good or bad, and the higher our conscious level, the faster we manifest. If you attach too much to an illness, you can bring that illness into your life. I always find that the best way to deal with it is to see the doctor, but I believe it's spiritual for me, and it always ends up spiritual. Don't get me wrong, sometimes fear kicks in and leaves me thinking about illness, and then I must realize that and remember that I am not my ego; I'm a spiritual being. In my own experience, if you take care of the chakras, you don't get ill more about chakras, further in this book.

The Dark Night of the Soul

The dark night of the soul or spiritual crisis often mimics depression. It is important to understand what a dark night of the soul is, as it will shed some light on why you feel the way you do. It will also help you make sense of your current reality. You are not going crazy; it's all part of the process. It does get better.

During the dark night of the soul, you will most likely come across ego death, or you may start to have a better understanding of what the ego is about. This needs to happen so that your soul can be reawakened and so you can be reborn into higher levels of consciousness, a new self!

It teaches you to embrace the darkness to find the light and become one with both. It's like a paradox where there's good, there's bad, where there is love, there is fear, and where there is dark, there is light, and so on... You must experience the loss to be able to gain. You must die to yourself so you can live. You must lose your way to find yourself again and walk your path. You must abandon yourself to find yourself.

I call this the caterpillar stage, as it's the stage between who you were and who you are becoming. The cocoon stage!! Soon you will fly!!

You will need to let go of your old self so you can emerge with the new, enlightened you. A lot of people enter the hermit mode during this stage while they are trying to figure out who they are and what their purpose is, which is what I did. They tend to shut off the world, but this is a healthy process and much needed for growth, as it's where inner work and healing take place. This is what darkness is about: diving into the shadow and pulling out what needs to be acknowledged and released. Your shining light onto it. It's about understanding yourself; what makes you think the way you do? It's an uncomfortable stage, but it's crucial for growth.

You may feel confused, angry, desperate, helpless, and lonely, but it's during this stage that things will eventually make sense for the first time. Remember that growth can only happen in your shitty days; growth cannot possibly happen when you're happy. This was a quote that got me through so much. So, each time you do shadow work, and you feel like the world is coming down on you yet again, remember those words because each time you pull out baggage from the shadows, you grow a little more.

You don't really need to do much in this stage, apart from riding with the waves, as it will be revealed to you in due time. Keep yourself in spiritual awakening groups and research a little on the dark night of the soul, and the universe will help you through the rest.

    The reason why the Dark Night of the Soul mimics depression is because of the symptoms, but in my personal experiences and my beliefs, there's no such thing as depression, and that is purely the Dark Night of the Soul which I came to understand once I researched about it and found the answer within myself that revealed to me the truth. Here are some of the symptoms of the dark night of the soul.

1. Loss of motivation
2. Extreme sadness with no explanation of why you are sad
3. No desire for sex
4. Poor hygiene
5. Loss of appetite or overeating
6. Problems sleeping
7. Crying a lot
8. Feel empty
9. Withdrawn from relationships
10. No interest in your hobbies
11. Thoughts of suicide
12. Nightmares
13. Body aches and pains
14. Feeling worthless
15. No energy
16. Digestive problem

Many people will seek a psychiatrist for depression and end up on antidepressants, as they are wrongly diagnosed with depression. The problem is not in your head; it is in your soul. That's why it helps to be in groups and do some research on the dark night of the soul and spiritual awakenings, so you can feel at ease and have a better understanding of what's going on. Everyone can experience a spiritual awakening differently, and it can depend on many factors, like your upbringing and whether you suffered abuse and trauma.

You can go through a dark night of the soul for a few months or for many years before a spiritual awakening happens. Your soul is calling you and has left you many voicemails, but until you pick up the call, your soul will continue to throw in the heartache until you listen.

Eventually, you will feel extremely grateful for the opportunity of the awakening and the dark night of the soul because it teaches you so much. However, it doesn't feel like a blessing at the time, but more like a curse. In Fact, it is a privilege that most people don't get to experience. They stay stuck in low vibrational states, repeating unhealthy patterns, or they stay in prison they have created in their minds.

There is so much to life than the work-eat-sleep pattern that you have been programmed to do. Knowledge is power, and the knowledge you need to know is important for transformation to happen. You hold the key to escape the suffering. The power is within you, and it's been there all along.

It's time to surrender and let it flow; stop resisting it. To surrender is to stop trying to control it, let it happen, let it flow, and trust that everything is working out in your Favour. There's a lot of peace in surrendering. Be kind and loving towards yourself, and watch the words that you say to yourself, as negative words will have an impact on the process. The brain is so powerful yet naive, and it will believe anything you tell it, so feed it well.

Give yourself permission to be where you are at, right here in this moment. Remember, the past has gone, and the future hasn't happened; none of which exists, only the here and now, and if you miss these moments, you will miss all the opportunities, insight, and messages that are presented to you to help you move forward.

Only be around people who serve your higher good. People who help you grow and support you. Switch off the news and declutter your Facebook from negative people and quotes, as this will only keep you in a loop and stop you from growing.

Keep meditating and pray to whomever that may be to you. I often pray to the universe, but some people pray to God, angels, and guides. It doesn't really matter who you pray to; the effects will be the same.

Try to keep your body moving, as this will boost your mood, as walking in nature. Sleep when you need to, even if it's during the day. You are not lazy; you are evolving, although it may not seem that way now. Sleep is where healing takes place.

Try to stay away from alcohol and caffeine during a dark night of the soul, as they keep you in a low vibration. Any food and drink that is bad for you should be consumed only in moderation, as we want to raise our vibrations and lower them. Play some good music that will lift your soul to help you vibrate on higher frequencies. Sometimes, I found comfort in the sad music as it helped me to get things off my chest, as tears are a form of healing and release.

Try to focus on positivity, especially positive thinking. I know it's easier said than done, but the reason we have dark nights of the soul is so we can work through the negative experiences throughout our lives and release them without putting too much attachment on them.

We cannot possibly be positive all the time, just like we cannot be happy all the time, but the idea is to not attach yourself too much to the sadness and try not to dwell on it. It's easy to attach ourselves to negative things when that's all we have ever known, which is why we need to give as much attention to happy things and less attention to sad things while finding that fine line where you're not bypassing the sadness but instead acknowledging it, feel the emotion then find a solution to help you feel better.

After the dark night of the soul comes the light, freedom, peace, a better understanding, and more self-awareness. This is where the magic happens; you tap into a higher power, and you become the creator. You can create anything you want. You're manifesting your dreams and bringing them to reality. There's no stopping you now!!

I'm living my dream as a writer. I love every moment of life, and I never take one second of it for granted. You, too, can do so long as you are taking steps forward. You will inevitably get there, but patience is the key and always take small steps because before you know it, everything else as effortlessly fall into place effortlessly.

Stages of A Spiritual Awakening

Dolores Cannon was one of my favorite spiritual teachers while on my journey, so I will use her stages of awakening because this was exactly the order it happened for me, but it doesn't necessarily happen in that order for everyone.

The Awakening

This phrase is often triggered by significant life events such as death or depression. You may have a sudden curiosity about life and its deeper meaning.

Seeking

Asking questions and getting curious about the world around you. A feeling that something is not right, like you have been lied to your entire life. Seeking answers.

Questioning

You begin to question everything

Like, why am I here? Who am I?

Self-discovery

Going inwards to find yourself. You may become a hermit at this stage, or you may crave to spend more time alone while you figure out who you are.

Healing

An urge to clean up your diet or exercise regularly.

An urge to do yoga or meditate

Integration

The puzzle is coming together, and experiencing more insight

You start to see how the lessons you have learned have shaped you into who you are today. You start setting boundaries that honour your growth. You are wary of who you let enter your life.

Service to others

As you grow and transition, you want others to feel that too, so you want to help others; you feel like it's your mission. Spiritual awakening isn't just about personal growth; it's about helping the collective consciousness.

Expand consciousness

Higher states of awareness, deeper connection to self, tapping into inner wisdom and knowledge. The world is filled with endless possibilities. You become curious with a sense of wonder.

Intuition and guidance

You rely more on inner guidance rather than external guidance, as your intuition is heightened.

Manifestation

You become the creator of your own reality. You notice how you are manifesting quicker.

Unity consciousness

We all connected

enlightenment

Peace, wisdom, and inner alignment

Oneness, connection to the universe.

This human in me

I have lived in many.

If only she could see

But she's reckless and careless

This human in me

I show her the way

It's frustrating, you know

This human in me

Has no clue where to go

The path that she follows

It is all over the place

It's cluttered and messy

It's a complete disgrace

I give her a nudge

And guide her at times

And when she is happy

I love how she shines

I am shouting so loud.

But this human is stalling.

She's in a deep sleep.

She cannot hear my calling.

So, you see

I had to do it

Because she was stuck

Throw in some heartache

To wake her up

I know it is cruel

To put her in this position

But she has a job to do

And that is her mission

When her mission is completed

She can simply be

For I can rest

With this human in me

Michelle Marriott

Learning to unlearn

I once heard a saying from Buddha: "Don't show up as the person you think you are; show up as the person you want to be."

This saying changed my life forever!

I had no idea who I was. I felt like someone completely different from who I wanted to be because I grew up with unnatural teachings that I became someone I didn't like. I didn't like the person my parents created. I was just plodding along, life lost and confused most of the time.

I took out my journal and got cracking on the person I wanted to be. Kind, compassionate, smart, empathic, creative, strong, powerful, beautiful, passionate, healthy, slim, courageous, brave, driven, motivated, focused, emotionally intelligent, and I focused on integrating those traits, but it meant unlearning a lot of crap I carried around with me.

The woman before was lonely, scared, not very smart, sad, fragile, timid, not very brave, unmotivated, lacked boundaries, unstable, weak, withdrawn, ugly, and fat.

I tried so hard to focus on becoming this woman by focusing on all those traits that I couldn't find in her. I didn't realise that it only took a shift in perception to realise that I was that woman all along. I had to unlearn the lies I told myself to see the woman buried underneath.

I then focused on asking myself some questions

What makes me think I'm not smart?

My father often told me that I wasn't clever enough and that I was something that stuck with me. Plus, I was academically behind in school, mostly because I couldn't concentrate, I was bullied, and the words from my father left an imprint on my self-esteem. Not to mention that school was not for someone like me because I knew from the start that school teaches you nothing, only lies.

What makes me think I'm ugly?

Someone once told me I look better with makeup on and that I was constantly comparing myself to others. What is the definition of beautiful anyway? I know I'm beautiful, and so long as I know that's all that matters. The opinions of others are not my concern.

Why do I feel lonely?

It was because the people I loved always left me, but so what? I love "me, "and that's the best feeling in the world to love yourself unconditionally, and that's all that matters. I live alone, but I'm far from lonely because I love my own company, and my thoughts are intriguing as they lead me to magical things.

Why did I feel timid and scared?

Because of the cruelty of people in the

world and what they did to me.

Do I see those people now? No, because it reflected the cruelty I placed on myself by self-harming, calling myself names like fat and ugly. Today, only nice people reflect on me, who make me feel good about myself and help me to grow, people who genuinely want me to succeed, not jealous people.

Why was I unmotivated?

Because I thought I wasn't good enough and that cleaning jobs were the only jobs I was good at. So, I stayed in my comfort zone. I believed that because I was told that, but here is me now proving everyone wrong.

My weight was hard to maintain because I would eat for comfort to relieve some depression, and most often, it was comfort foods that were unhealthy. I developed an eating habit tied to emotions.

I focused too much on what I looked like on the outside, so much so that I could never maintain my weight. Sure, I could lose weight for a little while but soon put it back on. It took another shift in perception to realise it's about what I put in my body, as to what it looks like on the outside. My body is not for other people's eyes; it's about how I feel living in it. My body is sacred; it deserves much more than an appealing eye. It deserves vitamins and nutrients. This is another example of self-love.

Once I uncovered the truth that this was all just rubbish, I carried into my belief system that clearly wasn't true, I discovered that the woman I set out to be was inside me all along and that my friend is authenticity!

The outside world has such a huge influence on our lives and perceptions that we fail to see this. We have adapted and accepted that what our parents, teachers, bosses, news, doctors, and government have all said is the truth set in stone that no one no longer questions anything, research things or even thinks for themselves.

I've always been one for questioning everything, that always got me into trouble, but why? What is wrong with asking questions? It's forbidden these days; I wonder why.

Transformation cannot possibly happen until we unlearn old things so we can find a way to learn new things. Letting go of old habits and beliefs so we make room for new ideas and replace old, unhealthy habits with new, healthy ones.

Unlearning lessons are about actively letting go of beliefs, behaviors, and patterns that no longer serve your higher good, so you can make room for new, aligned perspectives can grow on your spiritual journey.

As mentioned before, it's important to approach every situation with an open mind because, on this journey, you're going to find out that a lot of what you have been taught throughout your life is not true.

Look at it like this. As though you have just been born and you're learning all over again, a clean slate, forget about everything you have been taught, as well as everything you believed in and the stories you told yourself. Fresh start, new you!!! Now, ask yourself your question. What do you want your personality to be like? What would you like to create in your life? Keep the questions going.

Here is a little example of a story of mine. My mum, my nana, and her mum all suffered from bipolar disorder and schizophrenia. My nana was hospitalized several times, but somehow, something didn't quite sit right, and I often believed that what she was saying about ghosts was true. It's a hereditary condition, they say, so it had always been a fear of mine, and the fear stemmed from the fact that I, too, could hear voices, but I kept that quiet. I had always been fascinated by tarot cards, crystals, psychics, and spirits, but I was still a little skeptical about it all.

I went down the route of reading tarot cards and picking up energies from those who had passed and started witnessing things being thrown across the room and voices in my head. This scared the living daylights out of me, and all I could think of was schizophrenia and my nana being admitted to the hospital for her hallucinations and delusions. I tried so hard to switch it all off, but I always found myself drawn back into it. I was on the verge of being diagnosed with schizophrenia myself. I was exhibiting all the symptoms, and I can now see how it could have quite easily manifested that way.

I went to many psychic mediums who told me that I had the gift of a psychic. A part of me knew this, but I had no idea how to cultivate it without being scared. I didn't realise that in the spirit realm, there are still bad spirits as well as good spirits, and I was wide open to the spirit realm and was letting in bad spirits; these spirits mess with your head, hence the schizophrenic traits. I didn't know that you must learn to protect yourself and cleanse your home. I went my entire life scared of my own shadows and scared of my own gifts; I was running from "me."

When I started to love myself and embrace my gifts, I learnt how to understand them and that there is no such thing as schizophrenia and bipolar; in fact, mental health conditions don't exist, not in the way you think. I'm clairaudient; the gift of clear hearing is the same as my nana's.

Bipolar is the ability to create with the powerful energy that you have on a high, and the ability to do deep soul work on a low. It's a superpower!

Depression is your soul calling you to wake up! Haven't you noticed how people like Einstein and Isaac Newton have autism, ADHD, and bipolar disorder? They are all gifted! These are the people who change the world for the better. They never once let their gift be a burden; they stayed open-minded to all possibilities. That is where the power lies.

Once I realised this for myself, I was on my way too much bigger things. I was shifting blocks that were standing in my way from creating the life I've always wanted and following my dreams. That is what you need to do: be open-minded; the possibilities are endless. This was an example of what it means to unlearn something that you have learnt.

The chaos in her mind
Silenced her intuition
Her perception of the world
Cast shadows on her light

Silence is louder than you think.

And the light is brighter than you could ever imagine.

The outside world versus the inside world

What I found to be a good way to look at life is through the actions of others to get a better understanding of yourself. I see them as either mirrors, teachers or "add-ons" because the outside world reflects our inside world.

The more inner work you do, the more you understand this concept. Look at some of your past relationships and how they treated you. If they treat you unkind, can you see any parts of you where you were unkind to yourself? Do you speak unkind words about your body or the way you do things? If someone showed you no love, ask yourself, do you truly love yourself? The not-so-good parts, too. This is called mirroring.

This is not to say that you deserved any abuse that was inflicted on you. It's just saying that people and situations enter our lives to teach us something or wake us up from whatever it is we need waking up from. We just get so caught up in all the baggage and drama that we cannot see that.

If you find yourself in a situation where there is a heated argument that has gotten out of hand, and you're retaliating back at the unkind words that someone is shouting at you, it's a tell-tale sign that they are mirroring something deep within you. It's the retaliating back that gives it away. We cannot comprehend it because most people only know themselves on the surface. It is hard to see the deepest parts of yourself because they are tucked away in the subconscious mind. Unless you have explored deeper, you won't know what's in there.

On the other end, there's what is called projecting, and this is where people project their inner insecurities or inner shadows onto others. This is what people do, projecting and mirroring all the time.

So, if someone is shouting unkind words at you and you walk away without it affecting you, then you know that they are projecting their insecurities on you because you are familiar with your shadow work, and you have already done most of your shadow work. The more shadow work you do, the more this becomes clear.

In time, you no longer put yourself in drama situations because you value your peace too much. You can sniff out drama from a mile away; not only that, but your perception changes how you see people and the world. You no longer see drama, negativity, etc, it no longer affects you. Giving attention to the drama only attracts it back.

If you wake up grumpy, you tend to attract unwanted nuisances for the rest of the day.

Every Morning, I wake up and give myself a positive mantra like "Today will be a good, peaceful day" or "Today I choose to be grateful for the small things in life." It always works.

Questions to ask yourself

What are you reflecting on?

What would you want to shift and change within you?

Recognize that you cannot control everything, but you can control how you respond to the situation by shifting your energy and changing your attitude.

Shift your perception and focus on what is going well for you rather than what is going wrong for you.

Change your story

If you tell yourself, "I'm not good enough" or "Life is unfair," replace those words with "I am capable" and "I attract positive opportunities."

What emotions or beliefs are you holding onto?

Are you carrying anger or fear?

Journaling or meditating will help you understand these patterns.

Life does not happen to you; it happens through you. If we don't like what we see in the mirrors around us, it's a sign to look within.

When we approach the world with positivity, love, and hope, the world attracts that back to us.

```
A positive, loving woman who carries
compassion in her heart moved to a small
town. Her face lights up with joy,
happiness, and curiosity. She sees beauty in
everything. She sees the smiling faces of
wonderful people reflected in her. The town
comes alive with warmth and positivity. As
the woman goes home
```

She is left happier and content, convinced that the world is a beautiful, kind, safe place to live in.

A grumpy man hears about the town and decides he will move there as he likes what he hears. Skeptical but curious, he moves into his new home. He then takes a walk around the town with the usual frown he carries on his face, glaring as he looks around. All he could see were loads of angry faces glaring back at him. The man furiously shouts at them, only to hear them shouting back; he then gets into a fight. The man went home, and on his way, he muttered to himself, "What awful and angry people live in this town? That's it; I'm moving."

The town did not create those experiences; it simply reflected what the man brought with him.

It's always a good idea to approach situations from the heart and understand that others need healing, too, but that doesn't mean you have to stand for their projection. This is where boundaries come into it because those who don't serve your higher purpose and do not support and help you grow should not be in your life.

Of course, your children are different in this situation because when you do your inner work, your children often follow your pursuit. Children often seek attention from our reactions, but when we stop reacting, we start to see a shift in their behavior, too.

There are not only people who show up in our lives as mirrors, but so do situations. Losing a home or a job can teach us something: you must look at a situation and ask yourself if you can do something about it or if it's out of your control. Look at everything and ask yourself questions. Situations and people can often serve as messengers; I often call the angels in disguise.

I went through a period where I lost my home and all my belongings. I came back to the original town I grew up in with only the clothes on my back. My two boys lost all their toys, and I was in a mess.

I found myself a property and soon started to build back up and ended up in a much better place with a good job and better well-being.

Sometimes, we must lose to gain, and that saying stays with me because if I ever come across a similar situation, I'm aware that the universe is removing what no longer serves me and putting me in a better situation.

The people who project wish them to heal and move on because their work is done, but if you're still retaliating, these mirrors will only show up in different people until you learn the lesson.

Some people would argue and say that focusing on yourself is a selfish act, and over the years, society has made us believe that. It's the outer world that keeps us in that loop in the first place. In fact, it's far from a selfish act.

Of course, we are not saying that you buy yourself a coat before your own child, but instead, you're prioritizing your mental health and well-being to take care of those around you. Plus, others will follow the pursuit. That is how you shine your light from within. Here is an example.

My son suffered from depression, anxiety, anger issues, and social anxiety and didn't leave his bedroom for years. He was home-tutored due to bullying at school. He's autistic and has some moderate physical disabilities. His mental health was deteriorating so much, and I couldn't get him into the doctors as the lockdown from the global pandemic made it difficult.

I took up some courses on CBT therapy, which I already knew quite a lot about from the counselling and psychology courses I did back in the day, when I was studying between my depressive episodes.

No matter how much I tried to help him, nothing was working. That was when I removed myself from trying to control the situation and focused on my own healing. At times, I felt guilty for doing this because it just didn't feel right to be focusing on myself while my son was suffering. Of course, I would ask him if he was ok and be a pair of ears to listen to, but I often found myself giving him advice that he didn't want to hear. The techniques that I was using for my inner healing were working, and I wanted my son to have that knowledge to do for himself.

A year into my healing, I started to notice huge changes in my son. He started to do inner work himself, practicing breathwork and meditation and researching techniques that worked for him. He started going to clubs a bit more, his temper had mellowed out, and he seemed much happier than before.

He participates in spiritual practices like sound healing. Not only is my son following these practices, but other people around me are doing the same. When you shine, those around you shine, and that's how it works. You create a ripple effect!

Making different healthy choices and healing yourself allows you to create a different future timeline, one that is better and healthier.

The more inner work and shadow work you do, the more the mirroring will stop. Eventually, teachers show up; as the saying goes, "when the student is ready, the teachers appear," and that they did. This is when the magic really starts to take place because once the healing takes place and you're out of the "loop," there's no stopping you! And this is when you start to notice the "add-ons." These are rare gems because these are the people who "add" to your existing love and happiness that you have already found within.

Moving past the loop

We don't realise the power we have over our own minds and how our belief system hijacks us and keeps us in prison we have built within our minds. The reason why we are stuck in a loop and cannot move beyond our past is that we are not listening to what our soul is telling us. It wants us to acknowledge our past and understand it; it wants us to feel the emotions rather than push them away, but we are too afraid to do this because it's too painful.

Some people say that we must forget about our past to move on, and while this saying is partly true, it needs to be worded better, and it causes more pain than it does good. Instead, what we should be doing is understanding what our past is trying to tell us before we can let it go.

As mentioned before about my diagnosis, prior to that, I had been searching all my life for answers as to what was wrong with me, but I failed to see that there was nothing wrong; I was different, and it wasn't meant to fit in, as being different was my gift. Having the diagnosis of bipolar felt like a relief, but it just became a crutch that I used as an excuse for why I felt the way I did. On the days I was low, I was just riding it out as part of my bipolar disorder rather than doing the shadow to understand why I felt the way I did. I just assumed that the pattern of lows was one of the bipolar symptoms and something I couldn't change, so I wasn't getting to do my shadow work. I embodied it into my belief system.

Even those without bipolar and still finding themselves going through this loop, still wanting to find answers as to what is wrong with them, instead of trying to heal from the pain. Our focus is always on finding what's wrong with us... We think that we can just push our pain to our subconscious and forget about it because we told to, we told to forget about the past and move on, but doing that only keeps the loop going because we cannot possibly move on until we face our shadows as the only way past the pain is " through it's the only way to get to the light. Like the paradox, to experience the light, you must experience the darkness.

So, you are perhaps wondering how we get out of that loop, right? So first, I'm going to go through some types of things that people say when they are stuck in the loop...

I can't do this anymore.

You don't understand what it's like for me

It's not that easy

I've done everything, and nothing works

It's too late for me

I'm too tired to fight

And then there are the memes and quotes that people engage in on Facebook, not realizing how the Facebook algorithm works. What you share on Facebook, then Facebook will bring more tough quotes.

The words that you are speaking to your brain are then embodied into your belief system. You automatically believe it without even thinking about it. The brain does not know the difference between what is true and what is not true. You can feed it with any mumbo jumbo, and it will be believed. There's power in your words. Words can create, or they can destroy.

As mentioned before, about your mind being a prison cell, it's the words that feed your mind that keep you in the loop! So, you need to change the words you speak, so you might say, "It's not as easy as that," but it is as easy as that! You can quite easily say, "I can do this." Now, it doesn't happen overnight, so you will need to be consistent with it.

Positive affirmations have some amazing results, and just posting one positive affirmation on Facebook will get the algorithm going and start rewiring your brain. If you don't often go on Facebook, you can try posting sticky notes around your house with positive words on them. I will go through some more tips in the rewiring of the brain section.

Before we go any further, you need to ask yourself, are you ready? Are you prepared to put in the work? Because it won't be effective if you don't put in the work.

When the body stays in survival mode, it constantly keeps you in fight or flight mode, and this is when you feel a need to constantly protect yourself. In survival mode, a person can feel irritable or impulsive. In victim mode, a person may withdraw, complain, or seek sympathy. Victim mode is a mindset where you feel powerless and blame external factors for your problems.

The effects on the body when in constant survival mode create a state of chronic stress that can impact your inner peace and spiritual growth, leading to physical manifestations like digestive problems, headaches, and weakening of the immune system. It can affect your ability to be in the present moment and be mindful due to the constant state of high alert.

Engaging in relaxation techniques, getting enough sleep, breathwork, and regular exercise can help. Acknowledging your situation and prioritizing self-care practices is vital for your health.

When constantly stressed, the body releases high levels of cortisol and adrenaline, disrupting the hormone imbalance and overall well-being. Being in a constant state of anxiety affects your judgement, making it difficult to connect with your inner wisdom and clarity needed for spiritual practices and growth.

Breathwork allows you to step into the present moment, away from the stresses and instantly reduces anxiety. That's why when you take a deep breath and sigh, it instantly feels good.

Most people don't realise that they are breathing wrong; they take breathing for granted because it is an automatic thing, so they don't have to think about it, but what often happens is they start to breathe from the chest instead of the belly, and this causes problems in the upper back.

Find a quiet space to relax with no interruptions and place one hand on your belly and one hand on your chest.

When breathing in, the belly should expand out, and when exhaling, the belly should contract in, like you're blowing out a candle.

The chest should not move at all, and this will help fill up with more air, allowing you to breathe better and take pressure off the ribs and upper back.

Also, spending time in nature will help relax the body, as nature holds a natural ability to heal.

Further down in this book, I will talk to you about shadow work, how to rewire the brain by using positive affirmations, the benefits of breathwork, and so much more!

I don't want to overwhelm you too much, so it's important to remember that I didn't incorporate these things into my life all at once. I started with very small changes at a time, but those small changes put all the big stuff into place effortlessly! If you focus on big steps, you set yourself up to give up too soon, as it's challenging and overwhelming. That's why it's the small stuff you focus on first. For me, it was clearing out Facebook and turning the news off, as it was a time when the global pandemic was happening.

During the course of this book, I will go through a series of self-help techniques that will help you on your healing journey, many of which have been proven by myself and many others to be affecting, but sometimes it can be trial and error as to what works for you as it's always good to explore with different techniques to discover what works for you.

THE WARRIOR

I have uncovered the layers one by one

To be the woman I have now become

It's been a tough ride

With its twists and turns

Still, lots to look forward to

And a lot to learn

In my darkest days, I've no need to hide

I embrace it with love

And I wear it with pride

Nothing is ever what it seems

I am neither here nor there

I'm in between

The beautiful light

That captured my eyes

Helped me to see

And become so wise

This damaged, tired, worn-out vessel.

Has fought the battles

So, my soul could settle.

So, I gather my evidence.

And take with me my proof.

In search for my answers

And my ultimate truth

My fight is over

This warrior wins

My past is done

And my journey begins

So, I will take a deep breath

And one big sigh

And wait for that day

I can finally fly.

Michelle Marriott

Into the subconscious mind via dreams

Dreams hold a lot of significant messages and hold the key to healing. I got to find out so much of what was hidden in my subconscious mind by doing dream work and documenting them in my dream journal. This was a huge help during shadow work as it helped to identify and understand my hidden trauma and how it was affecting my mind, body, and soul.

It's difficult to start with trying to decipher the messages and symbols in your dreams, but I find that keeping a dream journal allows you to recognise patterns and eventually put the puzzle together.

Not only do dreams carry messages about your life, but you can also have visits from angels, spirit guides, and spirit animals, as well as gods and goddesses.

I was often visited by my nana, who is in the spirit realm, and she would enter my dreams, bring messages and sometimes just sit with me. She would often guide me, even when I was not dreaming, by sending me messages in my waking life. Often showed up just at the right moment when I needed her, and I knew from the cigarette smoke that she was there.

Before my nana passed, she was always the one in my life who gave me a bit of attention and love. Every Saturday, she would come to visit and bring me a gift, and every Tuesday, we would go to her house, and again, she would give me a bit of pocket money. In fact, the only toys I remember from my childhood were the toys my nana brought me.

One night, I was dreaming about this strange Gitty. I remember feeling curious as to what was at the other end of this Gitty. It was one of those strange dreams where you are an adult in my dream but still living at home with my parents. I was living at the house I grew up in, but on an unfamiliar street.

Out of curiosity, I walked up the Gitty, and I remember it being long. When I got to the other end, I found myself surrendering to fog; as I made my way through the fog, it started to clear a little. I looked behind me, and the gitty had disappeared, and I was left alone in what looked like an abandoned city. You could hear a pin drop! There were no people or even animals.

I sat down on what looked like a heap of cobbles and started to cry. I felt so alone and numb at the same time; crying was all I could do. I got up and started to walk back to see if I could find the gitty, and I could not see it when suddenly, a figure appeared, and it was my nana waving at me. She stood where the gitty was guiding me back out. I then woke up.

It wasn't until I started my healing work that I understood what this dream meant. Of course, it represents what is hidden in my subconscious brain. The feelings of loneliness and fog represented my conscious brain, as everything felt like a fog. The long gitty represented the path I was on at the time, and it was a long road before healing took place at the time of the dream; I was only 23, and my spiritual awakening was at the age of 45.

I often wondered what I would discover if I had explored the rest of the city and what I may have found.

I didn't realise that when a loved one visits your dream who has passed and you remember the dream in clear detail, it's because it wasn't a dream, and in time, I found this to be true. After that dream, I wrote my first poem, which was dedicated to my nana. After that, I continued to write poetry, and the poetry led me to write books... It was a good way to deal with and make sense of my emotions.

When my nana passed away, I was heartbroken and devastated because I lost the only person who was there for me.

Another dream I had was about a school, and to me, the school represents learning lessons and not just math and English lessons, but life lessons. I was in, again, a strange dream where I was an adult, dreaming of the school I went to and showing up as though I was 14 again. Same principle, no teacher, no pupils, just me. This time, I had two choices: I could go through the back gates that led into a quiet countryside, or I could go through the front doors where there were wars going off and bombs falling everywhere. Both led me home. Each time, I chose the front door, dodging the bombs on my way home.

I was too scared to take the back road because I was frightened of being alone and frightened of the unknown. The front gates were familiar to me. Again, I often wondered where those country lanes would take me. I know now, of course. I did set a reminder to myself to pluck up the courage and explore the countryside, but I didn't have that dream again. But I did, however, have other similar dreams.

The most recent dream I had was a visit from my last partner, who had sadly passed away. He was the only one who never abused me. In fact, he was completely the opposite, but he had many inner demons of his own to battle, and unfortunately, although I tried to help him, I had many demons myself to battle, and he was not ready to face his shadows. However, he continues to show up for me in my dreams, and every so often, he sends me messages from the spirit realm.

I dreamt that we were in this car, and he was driving. We came to what appeared to be giant monster trucks. I must laugh because, in waking life, he was obsessed with monster trucks and motorbikes. In fact, he had a couple of monster trucks and a KTM dirt bike that he would often take to the nearby field. I can see why he used the monster trucks as symbols. In my dream, these monster trucks were huge! There were three of them in total. The traffic warden waved us to drive under the truck. It was stationary, of course, but each wheel was twice the size of our car!! We managed to drive under and then came across a transparent, icy road. We managed to drive through and back onto the country lanes. Phew!

As you can see, he was showing me my path, as roads also represent your path, and the trucks represent my obstacles. The icy road represents the possible danger if I don't deal with my obstacles. Of course, he was telling me that I could get through it as we did in my dream. There were bits and pieces after that, and they will perhaps come to me in due course.

Although there can be many interpretations of the meaning of these dreams, the way to decipher them is to look at your waking life and use that as a guide to interpreting the dream, as your intuition will tell you which interpretation is right.

All my life, my dreams were about wars, but today, they are mostly about hospitals, trains, and schools, representing the healing journey and learning life lessons, and the train represents how fast I am reaching my goals. It's funny because I used to have more stops or train crashes, but now my train tends to run more smoothly.

Keeping dream journals was one of the best tools I used for healing, as it helped to understand what was happening in my subconscious mind, but it's not always easy to remember your dreams at first.

The best way to start remembering your dreams is to set an intention to remember by writing down in a dream journal, "I set an intention to remember my dream." Then, when I wake up, I would still write down even if I didn't remember; I would write, "I don't remember my dream today." By doing this, you're waking up part of the brain that is responsible for remembering. Sometimes, it comes to you later in the day, but sometimes it can take a few weeks to remember. In time, you will remember every little detail, and they will be so vivid.

If you have a nightmare like I did in the past, place a dream catcher above your bed and bless it every so often with some good, powerful words. I haven't had a nightmare since I placed the dreamcatcher above my bed.

However, I find that nightmares are a way of shouting at you when you are ignoring the messages your dreams are sending you.

During my journaling, I discovered I'm a witch. However, I don't practice in the way that most witches do. I consider myself a cottage witch because I bring magic into the mundane by setting an intention with everything I do. So, during my dream work, I placed a mugwort herb in a little pouch with an amethyst crystal and used the power of words to cast a spell to help me remember my dream, and it always worked. You can use whatever words you like because it's the intention behind the spell.

I tend not to practice witchcraft these days because I know that the power is within us, but that doesn't mean I don't do the odd tarot reading and play about with my crystals, as I still love my little trinkets.

What is shadow work, and why is it important for spiritual growth?

The shadow self is the parts of ourselves we don't like or the parts of ourselves we neglect. Everyone has a shadow side. Even if you had a good upbringing, you still have a shadow side. It can be difficult to attend to every aspect of yourself, especially when life can get so busy. That's why it's important to check on yourself regularly with questions like "How do I feel today?" so you can reflect on your emotions and help you identify anything lurking in your shadows, so we can bring forth and shine some light on them.

It's crucial that you have support in place if you are doing shadow work for the first time, whether that be a therapist, a family member, or a trusted friend. During the healing process, you might experience some uncomfortable sensations in your body, like unusual aches and pains that you haven't experienced before, or perhaps you get a headache. It's important to write all your experiences down in a journal so you can go back to it later, as you may see patterns or sudden insights.

You might also uncover some memories that you didn't know happened, and this can be alarming, but that is ok, and you must remember that it's all part of the healing process, and it will get better. Acknowledge the memory and the feeling attached to it. Try to make sense of it, and it's ok to cry, as crying is healing, too.

Once you have made sense of it all, you will need to realise. I find that writing it down on paper and then saying, "I erase this memory from my mind," then you will need to feel the memory slipping away by visualizing it, leaving every part of your body. You can also burn the letter as a final way of saying goodbye.

You may start to feel as though a weight has been lifted off your shoulders in just the first release. As time goes by, you will notice a little bit more come, and when it does, repeat the steps.

The more you do, the more you feel lighter and the less pain you will feel. You will start to feel much happier within the first few months, but it can take time to fully release the emotional baggage you have been carrying.

Always praise yourself for the healing you do, as this will help you feel good about yourself.

There may be times in between when you will struggle, and this is where you need to speak to your trusted support. For me, it was the spiritual groups on Facebook because we were all like-minded people, and they felt like my soul family, as I didn't have many people around me at the time who I felt safe talking to.

The dark night of the soul and shadow work is the hardest part of the spiritual awakening, and that is when I felt grateful for Facebook because we need like-minded people when on a spiritual awakening journey, so we don't feel alone. It's surprising how many awakened souls are just like us. In fact, all those who said I was weird have now become the weird ones to me.

The rollercoaster

Before shadow work

Once again, the battle begins

On the way to hell

And committing the sins

Another level

Has passed my head

Dangerous thought

getting out of bed

Back to reality

Where has the time gone

The rollercoaster keeps moving on

I never know how I will feel

But deep inside

I pray it will heal

Will it end

I don't know how

But at this moment

I'm happy for now

After shadow work

Once again, the battle begins.

On the way to the shadows

To see what draws in

Another level has entered my head

Forced to do inner work

Tucked up in bed

There's something to learn

I feel in my heart

Discovering more

This is where growth starts

I never know how I'm going to feel

But deep inside

I know it will heal

Will it end

This rollercoaster of mine

I sure hope not

For it helps me in time

But it's ok

I need not know how

But at this moment, I'm sad for now.

Michelle Marriott

The wounded inner child

To move forward and step into our power, we must first understand what inner child healing means and why, after all this time, we should open those wounds. Are we not supposed to forget and move on, you might say? Absolutely not!! Those deep-buried wounds are the reason why you struggle today.

Perhaps your childhood was great, and you had a fantastic upbringing with parents who loved you dearly, but that's not to say that you didn't develop fears and anxiety. Maybe you went swimming with your friends one day and had a terrifying experience where you almost drowned, and it frightened you so much.

It caused deep-rooted fears around water.

Perhaps you almost got hit by a car, but as years went on, you had forgotten about the whole experience and locked it away in your subconscious mind.

Today, you have anxieties and fears around water. You would love to soak in a bath or take your children swimming, but your fears and anxieties are too much to cope with. Your heart pounds every time you cross the road, and later in the day, you're feeling exhausted and drained from all the anxiety.

People often think that inner child work is only for those who have suffered child abuse or those who have suffered huge, significant traumas, but what we often forget is that what appears small and insignificant to an adult is huge and terrifying to a child.

Our childhood has a huge impact on our lives as adults, and although it may not affect us mentally, it can certainly affect our bodies.

My bladder problem today stems from the abuse in my childhood that is tied to my emotions. My hunch at the back of my neck is from the years of looking down because of depression that was rooted in childhood. And the severity of my self-esteem about what other people thought of me.

To work on your inner child, you first need to find a quiet space where you will not be interrupted. Close your eyes and think of the earliest memory, any memory you want to go back to. Say hello to your inner child and ask how she is. Wait a moment and feel whatever emotion comes up. Does she look sad? Perhaps ask some questions or see if she wants a hug. Tell her how much you love her and how amazing she is.

What emotions pop up? What thoughts enter your head? How do you feel? What do you see? What can you smell? Help them to feel safe and let them know how important they are So you have an idea of how it works. Below is a letter I wrote to my inner child while I was healing.

Dear Shelley,

I hope you like the cute unicorn journal and stickers I brought you, as I know you would have loved something like that. I just wanted to see your little face light up.

I want to let you know how much I love you and that I am so proud of you. You're an amazing, beautiful soul who is kind, compassionate, loving, and strong. Please don't stop being kind because the world is cruel, and don't stop giving love because you never had it.

There's a reason you went through this darkness, and that was so you could shine your light. You always wanted to do amazing things and change the world, and that is what you are doing.

Never think you are worthless and not loved, because you are loved more than you know. Shine your light; my love for the world needs you.

All my love.

Your letter can be written in any way you like, so long as your words are from the heart.

During my shadow work, I had to heal the wounded inner child, and the first thing I did was visualize the earliest memory as a child. I would visualize myself sitting with her and just observing and listening, and then I would offer her hugs and tell her how much I love her and that I will be back. I wrote my experiences in my journal.

One day, while walking to a charity shop, I was drawn to a unicorn snow globe; I took one look at it and said, "Why on earth would I want a unicorn snow globe at my age? And came home. The following week, I went back to the charity shop and saw that the same unicorn was still on the shelf. This time, I knew it was a call to buy it, so I did and came home. I sat down, looking into the globe as I shook it and found myself in a deep meditative state. At that moment, I was in a magical land where fairies, mermaids, dragons, and unicorns lived. As I opened my eyes, I was in awe at what I had just witnessed. I felt that I was in another realm; it felt so real. I had always had a very limited imagination, or so I thought, but it appears that I had unlocked a huge portion of my imagination. I saw the world through a child's eyes for the first time. I had to grow up fast, so I missed out on so much of my childhood.

A few days later, I was drawn to making a nature journal and ended up making two. I sat down writing about nature as I do when these words popped out of nowhere: "An adventure to birchwood bark," I intuitively wrote on the front of my 2nd book, representing a title. I remember thinking, "Did I just really write that?"

At that moment, I knew that my inner child had emerged with me; she came out from the shadow and was no longer hiding.

The next thing I did was look up to the universe and say, "I surrender." I was practicing my surrender techniques after reading the surrender experiment by Michael Singer, where you let go of control and follow the signs of the universe and your inner compass. I made the vow to the universe that the book would only be written in a moment. As I put pen to paper without thinking, these words just started to flow through me effortlessly!! And that was the day my book was born. Each day, I would take myself into nature and write. The book is a calibration with the inner child and the higher self.

We don't realise how much we need our inner child, even as adults, for creativity and imagination. Attending shadow work is one of the most important things I do even to this day, and although shadow work can be painful and uncomfortable at first because no one brings ups traumas and abuse and parts of ourselves we don't like, there are also gifts and talents hidden in that shadow, and in time it becomes a lot less painful, in fact, I look forward to doing shadow work! Don't get me wrong, sometimes I get my sad days like any other, but my perspective is different because I know that it's a growth period.

There was one more thing I had to deal with, and that was forgiveness. Forgiveness is not what people think it is. It isn't consoling what someone has done. You're not making up over a coffee. In Fact, you don't have to ever see them again. Forgiveness is for your own purposes. It is so you can release yourself from the burdens of resentment and anger to allow room for inner peace and spiritual growth. This was the hardest part for me on my healing journey, but it was so worth it in the end. This was when I felt another shift that allowed me to move on to the next part.

To practice shadow work, you must first be willing to explore the shadow self, even if you're not. Find it uncomfortable and scary. It's also very important to have support in place, whether that be a therapist, a family member, or a trusted friend; for me, it was the spiritual groups on Facebook.

Ways to practice shadow work include. Dream Analysis helps us to dive into the subconscious mind to see what's been suppressed deep within us by keeping a dream diary and looking for repeated patterns and symbols to see if you notice aspects of yourself that you ignore or suppress. It can be hard to recall your dreams at first, so if you don't remember, you can still write in your dream journal, "I don't remember my dream today." That way, you're still setting the intention to remember. After a few weeks, you will notice that you start to recall your dreams again.

Shadow work can be challenging, but it leads to a greater sense of well-being and self-awareness. It also increases creativity and improves relationships. It calms down the nervous system and, in turn, reduces anxiety. It's also very important to be patient with yourself while doing shadow work and to accept and love yourself just the way you are. Remember, you were doing the best you could with what knowledge you had at the time. Praise yourself for even making the decision to change.

It is only when you step into the light that you can fully appreciate the darkness.

Quiet the mind with meditation.

When I first started to meditate, I got so frustrated with myself that I gave up on the whole idea of meditating. I thought that I had to switch off my thoughts altogether, and there was just no way I could do that. My brain is like an ADHD brain; it never switches off!

The more research I did on meditating, I found many different types of meditation, and it was just a matter of finding one that worked for me, and that was crafting, which was a form of focused meditation. I found it to be so relaxing and therapeutic, but I still wanted to try switching my thoughts, which I still cannot do to this day, so I came to the realization that it isn't for me.

Then I came across a post that someone posted on Facebook that rationed with me, and he said, "You don't switch off your thoughts. Instead, you become the observer. The idea is not to attach to your thoughts but instead let them flow past without judgement and attachment" that clarified a lot for me and started to try that form of meditating.

I brought myself to the present moment, and I then brought myself to what was going on around me. For example, I could hear my waterfall and children playing outside. I could feel the warmth on my face from the sun. I then closed my eyes and focused on breathwork and soon got to the place where my thoughts were, but as the man said, I let my thoughts flow. It was hard at first not to attach to them, but with practice, it got better. Don't get me wrong, I still struggle today, and it can take many years to reach that point of being in complete stillness, but I'm ok with that.

Here is a list of the different types of meditating

GUIDED MEDITATION

Guided meditation is a type of meditation that is guided by a soft, calm voice. They are designed to keep you focused on the voice rather than your thoughts wandering. This is the best type of meditation for those who struggle with their thought process. There are many guided meditations on YouTube that are as little as 10 minutes long. Explore the different types of guided meditation to find which one is more comfortable for you.

WALKING OR MOVEMENT MEDITATION

This is a type of meditation that is often done out in nature. It is a more mindful practice where you focus on physical aspects such as movement in your feet and being present in the moment. Tai chi and qigong are good for this type of meditation.

MINDFUL MEDITATION

It is more of a focus meditation. It often involves focusing on your breath, body, and mindful eating.

ATTENTION MEDITATION

This involves concentrating on a focus point, such as a mantra or breath. It's about redirecting to your focus point when your mind wanders.

SPIRITUAL MEDITATION

For connecting to a higher power or the universe

CHAKRA MEDITATION

A practice of balancing and opening the body's energy centers is called the chakras.

VISUALISATION MEDITATION

Involves creating images in the mind's eye to promote relaxation and calm.

MANTRA MEDITATION

Involves repeating words, sounds, or phrases.

To start your meditation journey, I would recommend starting with just 5 minutes a day, so you don't get frustrated and overwhelmed like I did. Choose the best time that suits you, whether that be early in the morning, after work, or at night. Try and stick to the same time each day, as it will be easier to form a habit that way.

Try to incorporate some calming rituals into your daily practice, like incense, essential oils, waterfall ornamental plants, or some soft meditative music to help you. I find that waterfall ornaments help me tremendously during my meditation practices.

Choose your meditation, and don't forget to play around with the different types until you find what suits you. I also like color therapy and knitting as a form of meditation. Once you find what suits you, then place yourself in a comfortable position and just notice your natural breathing.

Start from your feet by relaxing them. Work your way up, relaxing every part of your body. Unclench your jaw and just let every part of your body loosen up and relax.

You may not want to choose a meditation from the list; you may want to just sit in peace and practice loosening up your body, and that is great, too, as it's a form of meditation. Whatever suits you is what's important. The most important thing is to find time each day to relax.

Give up the search, you're looking in the wrong places.

Remember that it's never about the outside world, only the inside world, which includes love and happiness. How many times have you found yourself saying, "I'll be happy when I get a new job," "I'll be happy when I meet the right person "I'll be happy when I move house."

We blame our unhappy moments on outside sources. Sure, you can feel excited when that new relationship comes, or you feel at home in your new house and content, but how long does that last? Not long and then you're onto the next search to make you happy!! Search, search, searching all the time, but what if I told you that happiness is a choice you make to feel happy within, and all these extras are all your "add-ons" that I mentioned earlier?

Happiness is a conscious choice that you make each morning when you wake up. You choose to be happy regardless of outside situations. You can feel happiness while drinking your favorite herbal tea or relaxing while reading a book.

This is the happiness that is sparked within you; it's the happiness that no one can take away. It's happiness that's yours that you created. It's the happiness that stays with you. When you look for happiness outside yourself, and you lose it, you're left with the same old feeling of emptiness until you find your next happiness.

Most often, people take the small things for granted, and this is where it helps to practice gratitude by making a list of the small things you are grateful for. Learning to be in the present moment gives you permission to simply be. Try it now, give yourself permission to just say "fuck it," and feel the relief that those simple words instantly bring.

Set your intention to feel happy by saying to yourself, "Right now, I will feel happy," then smile as you feel the emotion. Make yourself your favorite drink and take just 20 minutes where you are not thinking about anything but this moment. Now smell the aroma of your drink with a deep breath in and take a mindful sip and really taste the flavors. Notice how peaceful you feel. Even though there may be activity going off in the background, you still feel at peace now that you have created a little bit of happiness without searching for it.

It's easy to take a 20-minute break, but often, we are still doing something like chatting on the phone with our friend or family member or having a coffee but thinking about the next task. It's surprising that a mindful moment can bring you happiness. With practice, you can do this while doing the pots, and it's surprising how washing the pots can feel good and not like a chore. Did you smile to yourself while you were mindfully sipping on your drink, as that amplifies the feeling? If you're not used to practicing mindfulness, it can take time to achieve it, but eventually, that is where the inner happiness comes from.

You don't fear heartbreak as much anymore because you know you can always go back to your happy place. Of course, you might feel upset when a relationship goes wrong, but it won't feel as bad as it did before you found your own inner happiness; when you work on setting boundaries and healing yourself, you won't put yourself in a position to be hurt because you value yourself too much to take on just any relationship.

So, how do we find inner love? By acknowledging that love is not lost, it's there within you right now, ready to be activated. Love is not something you seek. Love is something that is within you, and when activated, it radiates out, and you attract love to you instead of seeking it. Amazing, isn't it?

If you search for love outside yourself, you will always feel a void within. You can have the perfect partner and tell yourself about every day for years that your partner is great, but I guarantee that if you haven't accessed the love within, you will feel a void as though something is missing in the relationship or something isn't quite right. That's because that void can only be filled by you.

When you fall in love with someone, you are activating what's already inside of you. It's not the person that gives you that feeling, although they have helped you activate it; it's what's already inside of you. You can randomly fall in love at any given moment, but most often, fear stops us from doing that. We tell ourselves that love hurts when, in fact, it doesn't; it's the fear of abandonment or fear of rejection that hurts, so we shield our hearts.

When you next walk into nature, take a mindful moment again and take notice around you. Don't just look at things but really see what's in front of you. How do you feel? You see a bird, a cute little bird, don't just say it's cute and walk away. Really notice it, notice its little beak and the way it hops around the tree, notice how it looks at you with its tiny little face. Can you guess what the little bird is thinking? Really connect.

Eventually, with practice, you will start to feel the love rise from within, and once you activate it, it can no longer be taken away from you, just like your happiness, and you get to feel it all the time. Eventually, when you meet someone, it amplifies what's already within you.

It's important not to close your heart to love, as it is close to everything else around you. Instead, set your boundaries so high and know your worth. Don't settle for anything less than what you desire. You can fall in love until your heart's content; it won't hurt you, it feels amazing! But don't just fall in love with people, fall in love with birds, trees, and this present moment. This is what unlocks true happiness. Of course, you will have shitty days like anyone else, but you know you can always access this at any given time.

Someone somewhere needs to hear your story

Don't hide behind the shadows

For you are the light for others to see

What is grounding?

Grounding, also known as earthing, is a technique involving connecting to the earth's electrical charge by making direct contact with the earth's surface.

It is a therapeutic technique proven to relieve stress and anxiety, boost mood, and help with overwhelming feelings. It also allows you to center your energy and tune in to the world around you, allowing you to be more present in the here and now.

There are many ways in which you can ground yourself if you do not have access to nature. Here is a list of ways to ground yourself.

Surround your home with plants and natural elements like crystals and rocks.

Take some cleansing showers or baths and visualize the water cleansing you or place some herbs and Epsom salts in your bath.

Waterfall ornaments

Or some simple visualization techniques where you imagine that you are growing roots from your root chakra while you take some mindful breaths.

Use your five senses to notice things around you.

When someone is more grounded, they will be more mentally and emotionally balanced.

- More present
- Practical calmness in stressful situations
- Have much more self-awareness.
- Make better decisions without reacting impulsively.
- Someone who is ungrounded will act impulsively,
- Get easily distracted.
- Difficulty in focusing.
- Lose touch with reality and get lost in their thoughts, feeling disconnected from their physical body.
- Overly emotional.
- Lack of stability.
- Lose connections to their surroundings, including connections to the higher self. /Universe.

Grounding is one of the most important things to do on a spiritual journey. It is the key aspect for your overall well-being, and it's very difficult to move forward if you are ungrounded, as this will leave you stuck and unable to create your goals and dreams.

Why journaling is a powerful tool

I've always been one for journals when I was younger, but I stopped when I became an adult. When I was young, it was more of a diary I used to keep rather than a journal. For me, journaling is much more than putting pen to paper and writing; it's more powerful than that! I find that each time I write my questions, I effortlessly answer them, as it's a higher source where the answers come from, as we are connected to a higher power. Before I write, I don't know the answers to my questions, and then I must ask myself, "Did I really just write that?" This is what it means to have the answers within you, and that they have always been there. Journaling is one of the most powerful tools for healing and getting to know yourself on a much deeper level.

Journaling helps you to understand why you do the things you do. It is a tool that helps you recognise patterns of behavior that need addressing. It is good for regulating and understanding your emotions. You're not just writing words on paper; your intuition guides you with these words, so if you write a question, most often, you tap into your intuition instantly, and there go with your answer. There are many journaling prompts to use, and if you're not sure where to start, YouTube has hundreds of ideas so you can pick out what questions resonate with you.

Help understand yourself and improve your mental health.

Journaling provides a place to express your thoughts and emotions, allowing you to release some emotional baggage; you will gain more self-awareness and manage stress much better. It helps you to identify unhealthy patterns of behavior, as we tend not to recognise the everyday stresses and are always on the go. It can lead to better coping mechanisms and help you understand yourself better. It essentially acts as a tool to declutter the mind.

Achieve your goals

Journaling helps you to keep a record of your intentions, progress and challenges, which allows you to keep track of your achievements and identify where improvement is needed. It helps you to maintain motivation to reach your goals, and it acts as a tool to clarify, visualize and actively work towards your goals. Journaling allows you to identify any obstacles that are in the way of achieving your goals. By recording your actions and achievements, you can easily monitor your progress and celebrate them.

Here is a list of the many benefits that journaling can bring.

Recognise unhealthy patterns of behavior.

Because journaling provides a safe space to reflect in time, it allows you to identify triggers and reactions that relate to unhealthy patterns, which can be identified and worked on. Writing down experiences helps you to understand what you have hidden within. Recording your moods can help you see situations or people who trigger you. Putting your feelings into words helps you to process them and gain perspective, allowing you to analyze your reactions without being overwhelmed.

See where there's room for improvement.

Journaling helps you tap into your creativity and explore new ideas. Writing is a way of gaining perspective and new insight. Once you can identify problems and work on ways to overcome them, you leave room for creativity and ideas to flow.

Recognise your strengths and weaknesses.

By recording your thoughts and emotions and asking yourself questions, you get to find out so much about yourself on a deeper level, and when you can identify your strengths, you can focus on what you are good at and work on those strengths.

Track personal growth.

Allow yourself 10 minutes a day to start journaling. Choose which time of the day suits you and try to stick to the same time so it becomes a healthy habit, and you will get better results in time.

Help with fears and anxieties.

Journaling allows you to confront your fears in a more controlled manner, leading to a sense of relief and reduced anxiety. By writing down your fears and anxieties, you will feel the burdens that you can lift. Seeing it all written down can help you see a different perspective and can help you realise that they are not as bad and as overwhelming as you think, and this will give you a sense of relief.

Boost memory and critical thinking skills.

You are actively engaging your brain, which in turn will boost your memory; you're exercising your brain and organizing and converting information on paper. Freeing up space in your working memory and improving your memory ability. When you're writing about the past, you are actively trying to remember details, which strengthens the neural connections associated with memory.

Discover new ideas and perspectives.

Once you declutter your mind, you leave space for new ideas and insight to flow, kind of like a computer freeing up space so you can generate new ideas.

Help you understand that your thoughts and feelings are not who you are, but something you experience.

You are much more than your thoughts and feelings; you're more powerful than you think; in time, journaling helps you to recognise that.

Help to control your emotions and process them.

Writing your thoughts, emotions and feelings down will help you to make sense of them.

Reduce stress

You're releasing pent-up feelings when you write them down, which in turn instantly reduces stress.

Reflect on your experiences.

Sometimes, we are so busy with everyday stresses that we easily forget and get lost in our emotions, and we don't realise what we are doing or saying. By keeping a journal, you can reflect on your experiences and bring them to your awareness. In time, this will improve self-awareness.

Prioritize problems

Make a list and organizing your list into priority steps. Anything that is a priority is a good idea to follow in the morning, as you can become too tired in the afternoon from daily activities and are more likely to put it off.

Reduce intuitive thoughts about negative events.

Journaling helps you to recognise your thought pattern; by journaling, you are putting yourself in a mindful state, which, in time, allows you to manage your intrusive thoughts and not react to them.

Unlock your full creative potential.

As mentioned before, you free up space to allow inspiration and creativity to flow more effortlessly.

Find inspiration.

I often find that when I journal, I am having a conversation with my higher self. We are born with the wisdom within us, and that wisdom comes from the higher self. Journaling is a good way to connect with your higher self.

Journaling prompts

- What are my strengths?
- What are my weaknesses?
- What makes me happy?
- How do I feel today? (Important to check on yourself regularly.)
- What can I do right now to make myself feel better?
- What am I grateful for?
- What have I learnt recently?
- What's on my worry list?

- What are my goals this month?
- What would I like to change about my life?
- What's my vision for my future?
- Feel free to add your own.

Journaling doesn't have to be a long process, nor does it have to be handwritten; you can journal on a computer, which is a good way for those who want more privacy. By setting aside just a few minutes a day, you can reap the benefits just as well. Journaling can have a huge positive impact on your life! Starting with something small, I like to check in with my feelings every day by asking myself how I feel and letting it flow from there. If I am unsure of how I feel, then I would ask another question. Sometimes, I make plans in my journal, and other times, I write about my day, so my journal is sometimes a diary. There's no wrong way or right way, but it is a good idea to try and keep it positive. What I mean by that is, if you're feeling low and want to express that, that is ok but aim for questions like "What can I do right now to make myself feel better?" because it's about moving forward and not dwelling on the negative. Of course, we want to make sense of what we are feeling and why we feel that way, but we also want to find solutions to improve this.

I have come up with a list below of journaling prompts that I personally found helpful, but feel free to add your own if you wish.

The list goes on! It's also a good idea to reflect. I follow moon cycles, and the full moon is about releasing, and the new moon is for setting intention and manifesting something new. So, during the full moon, I would release any unwanted things that no longer serve my higher good. It could be people who treat you unkind, or it could be repeating patterns of unhealthy habits or even clearing out the closet. On the moon, I would set my new goal and work towards making it happen, no matter how small. It could be a small goal that works towards your bigger goal, but you must always remember that small steps are better than big steps to start with, because if you overwhelm yourself, you will give up easily. During the waning moon, I would use this time to reflect on the previous month to see where improvement needs to be and what I can do differently to make things happen. As mentioned before, journaling can be as little as 5 minutes a day for huge benefits or simply just checking in with yourself by asking how you feel.

. I journaled on my negative patterns of behavior and the repeated patterns of bad habits that had been passed down from my ancestor's line. However, it is true that when you heal those patterns, you break the generational cycle, and sometimes our past. Ancestors need healing, too. This is the transformation journey to seek and heal the generational traumas and patterns that have been passed down in our families. I set aside an altar just for my ancestors to let them know that healing will be taking place.

Each time I do more healing work, I feel an intense transformation. I unlock more.

Practicing self-love

Self-love is not just about placing some makeup on your face or dressing nice; it's much more than that. It's treating yourself kindly and being mindful of how you speak about yourself.

For most of my life, my self-talk was horrendous; it was mean and hurtful, and I was a bully to myself. Stepping back now and looking at some of the words I used to say to myself makes me feel ashamed of myself because I would never speak like that to someone else, so why do we do it to ourselves?

I'm fat; I'm ugly; I'm an idiot; I'm thick as two short planks; my body looks like an orange gone wrong. I'm so stupid. The list goes on. So why on earth do we do this to ourselves? I think most of the time, it perhaps starts as a joke and then becomes a habit, or in my case, I believe those words.

One of the best feelings in the world is loving yourself unconditionally! When I started to practice self-love, I looked at my words, and I have since then been a huge believer in the power of words, as I am aware that words can either destroy or heal. I started with words like "I am worthy of love." I then started with a self-care routine, but instead of just quick washes, I would take the time by placing rose petals in my bath and using rose quartz for self-love. I would then light a candle, and sometimes, I would read a book in the bath.

Each night, I would brush my hair and put on my creams, but each time, I would set intentions in my mind like "this cream will make my skin feel soft and give my face a glow." I would then make a cup of herbal tea, setting an intention: "This tea will give my body a boost of energy." Whatever my body needed, I would say while I was sipping mindfully on my herbal tea.

I decluttered my Facebook and got rid of any negativity. I would also surround myself with people who support me and motivate me. Anyone who was negative or made me feel bad in any way would no longer be entertained.

One of the best ways to love yourself is to gain confidence, and I found that body posture was a way to do just that. Standing straight, correcting my posture, and walking with my head looking up and shoulders back with a smile on my face made me feel more confident because all my life, I walked with my head down to the floor, and this gave me a hunch at the back of my neck. The more confident you feel, the more love you feel for yourself.

Don't lose yourself in relationships!

I often lost myself in relationships.

If you don't love yourself first, you will lose yourself in relationships

Find the good in every situation, and don't read too much into negativity.

Self-care isn't the same as self-love.

Self-care is taking care of your mind, body, and soul by eating healthy, exercising, meditating, and doing the things you love to do. Have fun or read books. Do something creative. Push yourself out of your comfort zone by doing something you wouldn't normally do.

Give to others; when you truly believe that you're here for a purpose, loving yourself will come naturally.

Forgive yourself for the mistakes you have made and forgive others. This is not condoning what they have done.

If you don't love yourself first, you will lose yourself in relationships

Find the good in every situation, and don't read too much into negativity.

UNCONDITIONAL LOVE

To that special someone
You make my heart sing
I love the way you love me
And the happiness you bring

I love everything about you.
The good and the bad
You're beautiful in my eyes
May I add

As I look at you
And touch your face
You keep me warm
And I feel safe

At times, I get sad
And you're there by my side
With you, I am myself
I've no need to hide

I'm truly blessed

I know you know

You stuck by me

And helped me grow

There is no one who knows me

Quite like you

You have seen the deepest parts of me

That I never knew

The love and happiness

I no longer seek

As we worked so hard

Your love, I keep

I can now fill the void.

And finally, rest

No more searching

For I am whole and blessed

It seems like forever.

Six years ago

When you showed up

To say hello

I will never forget it

As we made that commitment

You loved every part of me

Without any judgement

So, I open my heart

To this person in my life

I've never felt so loved

And more alive

I can look in the mirror.

And I am grateful to see

This profound love

Staring back at me

Michelle Marriott

The ego

The ego is the "I "who you believe yourself to be; what beliefs to carry about yourself? Your personality, your worth, your abilities. A lot of spiritual people believe that the ego is not important, although some believe that the ego is like inner guidance, like our intuitions, as the ego lets us know when danger is around the corner; the problem arises when we let our ego control our every move.

In my own personal experience, we don't need the ego as guidance when we develop a good, strong intuition. The problem we have with the ego is when we allow it to take over our lives, and this is easily done if we're unaware of that happening.

The ego is neither good nor bad, but it can become one or the other depending on how much control you allow it to have over you. The ego can become dark when we get attached to it. The danger is that we become stuck in it, and it rules our lives. The real demon is clinging to the ego and the image of who we think we are. What we really need to do is first understand that you are not your ego, meaning you are much more than you think you are and capable of so much more than you think. When letting go of the ego, you become more compassionate with a greater connection to others. Not only that, but you have a deeper sense of peace and fulfilment.

During my spiritual awakening, I was practicing meditation, which allowed me to imagine myself as an observer of my thoughts, as though I were sitting in the back seat watching my thoughts from afar. I practiced watching them without placing judgement on them and without attaching myself to them. At first, it was difficult to do; in fact, I swore I would never be able to do it as I have an ADHD brain, and my thoughts never switch off! In time, it gets a little easier. I still struggle sometimes, as it can take years of practice to achieve. My biggest problem was that I got bored with meditating, and the whole idea is to find enjoyment in meditating for it to work efficiently. Once you start to reap the benefits, you will want to do it more often.

I would set my mantra and say, "I am not my ego." In time, I started to see the ego for what it is. When fear started to arise, I would take a deep breath and repeat my mantra again: "I am not my ego." The fear would again subside. This allowed me to gain control, and I could soon see that fear does not exist and that it's an illusion that comes from the ego. I started to see a different perception of who I was. I felt connected with everything and in unity with the universe. I gained a deeper sense of love from within and more compassion with everyone. The ego no longer dictates my perception.

To balance the ego is to understand that you are not your ego and to focus on self-awareness.

Avoid comparing yourself to others, as this gives power to the ego to take over again. Learn to embrace feedback, acknowledge your mistakes, and remember that no one is perfect. Everyone is on their own unique journey. It is important that you prioritize your own learning and growth over the need to always be right and better than others. Don't measure your worth against others, as this leads to feelings of inadequacy. Focus on your own progress and achievements.

- Be open to receiving constructive criticism and use it as an opportunity to learn and improve.
- Acknowledge your flaws; mistakes are good, they allow you to learn from them.
- Give compliments to others and recognise their strengths
- Be willing to change your mind when new information comes in.
- Avoid dwelling on the past and worrying about the future
- Avoid dwelling on your failures. Failures are good, and we can learn from them.
- Develop empathy, try putting yourself in other people's shoes, and understand their perceptions and experiences.
- Practice mindfulness to help you become aware of your thoughts and emotions, including ego-driven tendencies.

Ancestral healing

You didn't think healing ends with just you, did you?

A lot of what you must heal comes from your ancestors, traumas, illnesses, addictions, habits, and even your entire belief system!! It's passed down. From the moment you're born, you pick up input from your parents and, of course, from school and friends, none of which is " you," so it makes you want to question what part of you is truly you?" close your eyes for a second and imagine you had no parents, no ancestors, yeah I know hard to imagine but just hypothetically speaking for a second! Imagine, no baggage, no illness, no trauma, no addictions, just the purity of "you" purebred!! Let's say you just appeared!

Now, let's say you already know about spirituality, the chakras, self-healing, higher consciousness, and all the spiritual things. So, who are you? Have you worked it out yet? The clue is in what I wrote. You are a spiritual being living a human existence!! A being of pure love and light! It's your soul, pure soul! The rest is passed on and programmed into you.

We have the power to heal ourselves and others, including our ancestral line. We can become that pure being of love and light; in fact, we don't need to become one, we already are; we just need to clear all the crap that we have been carrying, the crap that's not ours to carry. Once we do this, we can then focus on what we came here to do, whatever that might be to you, because you didn't think that our purpose is to work a 9 to 5 job just so you can eat and work your ass off so you can go on a holiday once a year that's costing you your marriage and sanity because all you do is work, if you are lucky you might get to watch a half hour of your favorite serious. Absolutely not!! But a lot of people are stuck in this work-sleep-eat pattern!! I personally don't like to use the word "SHEEP," as most spiritual people call others who are oblivious to what's going on; I'm far too compassionate for that! We are all right where we are meant to be; we are either healing, learning lessons, or evolving. Some people struggle to face their shadows because it is too painful for them, or they surely don't want to and would rather take a pill to function each day. It's their choice, and there's one thing I've learnt is that you cannot interfere with another person's path because they could be dealing with karma. Who knows, we can plant seeds, though.

This is what all the inner work is all about on our spiritual journey. It's about healing ourselves, breaking unhealthy patterns by removing what's not ours to carry so we can become the love and light being we are. When we work on ourselves and break the cycle, we clear it for the next generation, so they don't have to carry the burden. There are many ways that we can heal our ancestry line; bear in mind this goes way back, so it is lifelong, but when we heal, we also heal the ancestry line.

The key to life

The deeper you go within
The more you see so clear
Messages all around you
Will suddenly start to appear

The depths of your fears
They are no longer tense
As your life unfolds
And starts making sense

Your senses are heightened.
Your power is turned on.
A new life begins
And the old one has gone.

Each day you
Are learning more
With the key in your hand
To open each door

Michelle Marriott

I can do this, says strength.

I know you can say hope.

What if I fail? Says ego

Keep moving forward, says wisdom

But I'm afraid, says fear

Keep learning, says knowledge

How says curiosity

Follow your heart, says intuition

When all else fails, sit back and take a deep breath. Life is too short to worry; it doesn't matter what you do so long as you do what you love with love in your heart, choose peace and happiness, and go with the flow of life, because no matter where life takes you, you will always end up right where you are meant to be, says destiny.

The importance of setting boundaries

Throughout life, I never had boundaries set for myself; in fact, I didn't even know what it meant to have boundaries in place. It was never spoken about with my parents. I spent most of my life just giving, seeing the good in everyone's and helping everyone. But all this did was led to everyone taking advantage of me, and I left, too afraid to stand up for myself. My upbringing did not help, but that's a story for another time.

Setting boundaries helps keep our body's aura and energetic field clear and healthy. Our boundaries keep unwanted energy, emotion, and pain from other people out of our energy system. I have learnt how much space I can hold for someone, as some people can drain your energy and life force out of you, leaving you depleted.

I'm also an empath, meaning I can feel other people's emotions and sometimes their physical pain. A little different from empathy, which is the ability to put yourself in someone's shoes, empaths literally feel others' pain and emotions, and they often take it on as their own, which leads to a lot of burnouts. Being an empath is an extraordinary gift to have because they can sense the energies around them, they are able to stay clear from dangerous predators, and they can make excellent counsellors for those in need, but if not recognized and understood, it can be a burden to carry because they literally soak up the emotions of others like a sponge! This is why empaths need good boundaries in place. Once boundaries are set, they can then start to embrace this amazing gift!

I remember saying "no" was hard to do, especially when your purpose is to help others, but I didn't fully understand the concept of boundaries, and I would feel bad for setting the boundaries. So, what are boundaries? It's communicating with your own needs and limits to others, saying, "This is what I'm comfortable with," "This is where I draw the line," and saying no when necessary. Attending to your own well-being while respecting others' boundaries as well. It's important to express your needs without feeling apologetic and maintain boundaries even when challenging. Choosing a time and place that is right for having discussions while maintaining respect for others.

Rewiring the brain

The brain is so powerful yet naive

It will believe anything you tell it

It takes time, patience, and consistency to rewire the brain! By using a variety of spiritual practices to change the neural pathways in the brain, we can live with a deeper sense of connection, peace, and awareness. Practicing things like positive affirmations, mindfulness, and meditation will allow your brain to adapt and change. By using these repeated experiences, you can train your brain to focus more positively. I understand that it is unrealistic to be 100% positive all the time, and there are always going to be times when negativity strikes but looking for more positive ways to deal with it rather than dwelling on the negative is the key.

Let's go through some of the tools I used to help rewire the brain.

Positive affirmations

Positive affirmations stimulate the neural pathways; this helps you to replace negative thought patterns with positive ones. This leads to changes in self-perception, improving mood and behavior by activating the brain's reward center. Repeating positive affirmations daily will improve stress and anxiety.

Meditation

Meditation reduces stress and anxiety, helps to improve focus even when you are not meditating, helps you become aware when your attention drifts, improve memory, become more present and aware of your thoughts, it can help you manage and control stressful situations better, improve sleep, help you to stay centered in your inner peace, manage symptoms of medical conditions and it boost the feel-good chemicals in your brain called the serotonin and dopamine's.

Mantras

Mantras work in the same way as positive affirmations; the difference is that mantras are considered sacred sounds and words with a spiritual significance that dates to ancient times. Affirmations are more personal, and mantras are focused on the vibrational power of sound.

Mindful practices

Studies have shown that practicing mindfulness reduces the grey matter in the brain region; this improves self-awareness, regulates emotions, and better decision-making. Like all the other spiritual practices, mindfulness helps with stress, improves cognitive function, improves sleep and overall leads to a calmer life.

Gratitude

When practicing gratitude releases the dopamine and serotonin feel-good chemicals in the brain associated with happiness and pleasure, enhancing your mood and again reducing stress and anxiety. Incorporating gratitude into your daily life can help you remove all other bad habits, such as overeating or spending habits, which are also responsible for releasing instant feel-good chemicals in the brain. Practicing gratitude can lead to a more optimistic outlook on life and, over time, strengthen neural pathways related to positive emotions.

Nature walks

Walks in nature can improve your mental health, creativity, and concentration, not to mention make you feel calmer and joyful. Nature can also make you think more clearly, reason more effectively, and solve problems. Spending time in nature will reduce stress, anxiety, fear, and anger, which in turn helps you feel more in control. It's a good time to reflect when walking in nature.

I discovered positive affirmations at the beginning of my spiritual awakening when I came across some spiritual magazines. One of the magazines came with a free pack of affirmation cards each morning; I would pull out a few and read them to myself, and then I would place them where I could see them. Sometimes, all over the house. I started on my journey with small steps. As you can see, so far, I started with removing negative people and situations as much as I could(unfortunately, I couldn't remove my son, ha-ha, only joking), to journaling and then affirmations, as I didn't want to overwhelm myself as it was a little habit, I tend to get myself into. We often speak so negatively about ourselves that sometimes we don't even realise that we are doing it. In my experience, the brain believes anything you tell it, so why not feed it a bunch of positive affirmations to get neural pathways going?

Meditation was a hard one for me, as my brain would never switch off! It took me ages to master what it was about, and I thought it was about removing the thoughts from your brain. I got so frustrated and found that crafting was my ideal meditation.

Then, I eventually came to understand that it wasn't about removing the thoughts but about not attaching yourself to the thoughts and getting carried away with them. Instead, you become the observer of your thoughts. It's like you're in the background, letting the thoughts just effortlessly flow without attachment. It does take some time to master, but giving yourself 5 minutes a day will give you so many benefits, from stress relief, improved focus and enhanced memory. It can also help with burnout and anxiety, reduce heart rate, better sleep, maintain blood pressure and many more.

Mindful practices are bringing your awareness to the here and now and focusing on what you're doing at the given moment. It's quite easy to physically clean the dishes while your mind is thinking about the next task. We always seem to be somewhere else other than the present moment. Spending too much time in the past only causes depression, and too much time in the future only causes anxiety. We don't realise that all our opportunities, messages, and intuition happen in the present moment, and we are missing them all.

Some of the things that helped me to be more mindful were getting in touch with all my senses by paying attention to smells around me, the sounds, and the textures. I would often do this out in nature, as I kept a nature journal, it's where I would go to write. I would jot down how many pictures I could see in the clouds. How many animal sounds could I hear? How many different trees I could see, just really getting in touch with my senses. I would focus on breathwork because there's nothing better than that for bringing you into the present moment. I would move my awareness to my body and listen to what it's telling me and practice mindful eating by smelling my food and really tasting it, noticing what it looks like, and chewing more slowly.

My next step was to practice gratitude. I find that being grateful for what you already have in your life brings in more. You feel much happier and healthier. I would write a list of all the things I was grateful for, no matter how small. I would notice all the things around me and appreciate them. Practicing gratitude can enhance empathy and reduce aggression, reduce symptoms of depression, improve sleep, and enhance self-esteem.

One of my favorites is walking in nature, especially if my mood is low, as it helps to boost my mood and leaves me stress-free! Being a writer, it's important for me to get out in nature, as it's where I get inspired, and it gets my creativity flowing. It also helps with concentration span, helping you to focus more.

In time, you will start to see more positive improvements in your well-being, and the brain takes on a more positive outlook. As mentioned before, this takes time and patience, and it's important to praise yourself for the small wins you achieve. I used to forget this important part because I was more focused on achieving the big stuff, as the small stuff was insignificant to me and went unnoticed, but all I was doing was focusing on the frustration of not achieving the big steps, and I would just give up! Once I started to praise myself for the small steps I was taking, before I knew it, the big steps flashed before my eyes as if they just leaped out of nowhere!! I found it helpful to write down all my small achievements where I could see them, so I could just keep adding and watch the list grow.

The mind is powerful.

You can feed it what you like

Just know you're in charge

And feed it what's right

Whatever you feed it

This is what you will receive

So feed it with the positive stuff

And you will achieve.

Michelle Marriott

ANGEL LOVE

When all hope has failed

And you have nowhere to turn

Call out your guides

And be ready to learn

Except for your destiny

With love and peace

Continue your path

Feel fear release

Know that you're loved

And guided each day

Together we stand

Together we pray

Your angel friends

Never leave your side

They will lend their shoulder

For the tears you've cried

Listen to their voice

When you are down in despair

It's their job to soothe you

It's their job to care

They will give you strength

To keep up the fight

Filling you with love

As they surround you with light

They will take you to places

Where you can feel free

So magical and bliss

Where you can just be

Be grateful each day

And hold on tight

For you are strong

You are loved

And you are light

Michelle Marriott

The forgotten chakras

The chakras play an important part in spiritual growth and were once a well-known thing in spirituality thousands of years ago. Chakras first originated in India. The chakras are intertwined with yoga, meditation, and breathwork. An ancient sacred knowledge dating back 1500 to 1000 BC. They are still used today alongside complementary medicine.

Chakras are energy wheels that run from the base of your spine to the top of your head and rotate when in balance. When the chakras become unbalanced, this makes you susceptible to illness. Maintaining daily spiritual practices like meditation, yoga, and breathwork will help keep your chakras healthy and in balance.

I first came across chakras 5 years ago at a curious point on my healing journey. It was one of those moments where my intuition was nudging me, so I spent long hours researching. I knew that one day, it was going to be a part of my purpose. I had always been told that my hands were like radiators, and in the past, I would often meet energy healers, as they were called back then. From a young age, I would often place my hands on my body where healing was needed to take place. I never really thought anything of it. Looking back, the breadcrumbs have always been there. I always say if you want to know your purpose, investigate your past, as it's where the clues lie.

As a young child, I always used to say that humans would one day live forever. I believed that so badly, and up until this day, I know they will one day. That is why learning about the chakras is so important for me, and not just me, but a lot of others on their spiritual journey understand and know the importance of looking after the chakra system. If we eat a healthy, balanced diet, exercise daily, sleep well, drink plenty of water, and balance our chakras, we will not get ill because illness has to break through our aura and into our chakras before it gets to our bodies, so if our aura is protected and our chakras are well balanced, then we don't become ill. This is why it's such sacred knowledge.

There are seven main chakras, and each has its own part to play. There are many more chakras, but the seven main ones are the most common. Below is a list of those common chakras and what each one represents.

Root chakra (colour red) - located at the base of the spine, this chakra is responsible for security, survival, and stability.

Sacral chakra (colour orange) - located just below the navel, responsible for creativity, emotions, and relationships

Solar plexus (colour yellow) chakra- located just above the navel, responsible for personal power, confidence, and self-esteem

The heart chakra (colour green) - located in the Centre of the chest, is responsible for love, compassion, and connections.

The throat chakra(colour blue) - located at the throat, responsible for speaking your truth, authenticity, and personal expression.

Third eye chakra(colour purple) - located between the brows, responsible for inner knowledge and consciousness

Crown chakra(colour violet) - located at the top of the head, responsible for connecting to higher power and enlightenment.

When chakras are out of balance, they can cause physical, emotional, and mental symptoms like pain, numbness, anxiety, depression, low self-esteem, feelings of disconnection, difficulty focusing, overthinking, procrastination, feeling unsupported, and difficulty making decisions.

For example, when the root chakra becomes blocked, we can develop things like arthritis, sciatica, constipation, eating disorders, and emotional imbalance relating to basic needs like money, food, and shelter. When balanced, you feel secure and grounded and can care for yourself and others.

A blocked sacral chakra can cause problems in the reproductive system, struggles in relationships, unable to express emotions, urinary problems, kidney problems, lower back pain, addictions, lack of creativity, hip and pelvic problems, and so on. When balanced, you feel comfortable taking risks and entering passionate relationships.

A blocked solar plexus physical symptom can show up in the stomach with digestive problems, chronic fatigue, issues with the pancreas, high blood pressure and diabetes, issues with personal power, self-esteem, and so on. When balanced, you have a sense of self-worth and self-esteem.

A blocked heart chakra can show issues such as asthma, heart disease, lung disease, and problems with the breast, upper back, and shoulder; you can feel anger, jealousy, abandonment or bitterness, and lack of self-love. When balanced, you have compassion for yourself and others and self-love.

A blocked throat chakra can cause thyroid problems, ear infections, laryngitis, neck and shoulder pain, lack of willpower, and issues communicating. When balanced, you're able to speak your truth and can easily express yourself.

A blocked 3rd eye chakra can cause headaches, blurred vision, hearing loss, seizures, hormone dysfunction, issues with moodiness, and self-reflection. When balanced, you have good, strong intuitions and can receive insight.

With a blocked crown chakra, you may struggle with depression, an inability to learn, sensitivity to light and sound and environment, and issues with self-knowledge. When balanced, you can tap into inner knowledge and connect to the universe or the divine.

I find qigong to be one of my favorite ways to unblock the chakras because if I don't have much time, I can do a 10-minute practice, which will help balance all my chakras. Other times, I love using essential oils and incense as it's a morning routine for me. I make essential oils mixed with a carrier oil, such as almond oil and place a few drops on the chakra that needs unlocking. Frankincense and lavender will help with the crown chakra. Peppermint and tea tree will help with the throat chakra. Rose and geranium will help with the heart chakra. Rosemary and patchouli will help with the 3rd eye chakra. Ginger and lemongrass will help with the solar plexus. Ylang-ylang and orange will help with the sacral chakra, and cedarwood and more will help with the root chakra. I mix a few drops of each in a dropper bottle filled with almond oil and use it when I need to. Feel free to make your own blend but always make sure you mix with a carrier oil, as essential oils are very strong and can damage the skin.

I also find nature very soothing for balancing the chakras; it instantly calms me, which is good for the nervous system, and breathwork always works a treat when you don't have much time.

Visualization techniques, using positive affirmations and mantras. The foods you eat are always important, like root vegetables for the root chakra, oranges for the sacral and yellow foods for the solar plexus, and apples for the heart. colour therapy using the colours of the chakras. I'm a very creative person, and that includes the clothes I wear, so regardless of the weather, I will still wear colourful clothes to represent my chakras. By keeping our chakras balanced, we keep our immune system healthy and our nervous system.

Inner work becomes quite addictive because the more work you do, the more powerful you become and the more empowering you feel. It's a lifelong healing.

The power of crystals

Crystals are naturally occurring materials and hold very powerful healing properties. They possess a unique energy and vibrations that can enhance well-being. They have been used for thousands of years by many spiritual teachers.

Crystals can help balance and align the chakras, which are energy wheels in the body. They can be used alongside meditation.

Each crystal vibrates differently and can be used to amplify your intention when manifesting.

Some crystals can be used for protection, cleansing the home, for travel, for your plants, and the list goes on.

Here is a list of the different types of crystals and their healing properties.

ROSE QUARTZ

Associated with love, compassion, and emotional healing. If you need self-love, place rose quartz next to your heart while meditating and use mantras like "I am loved," or you could wear a piece of rose quartz jewellery.

AMETHYST

A stone for spiritual awareness and intuition.

When you're feeling disconnected from your intuition, wearing an amethyst will help you connect back to your intuition. It also helps with tapping into your psychic abilities.

CITRINE

Promotes positivity, abundance, and creativity. It will also help you to find a job, so if you are going for a job interview, wear this gemstone for luck.

LAPIZ LAZULI

My all-time favorite was worn by my spirit guide (Isis, the Egyptian goddess). This gem enhances communications and brings you spiritual insight.

SELENITE

Known for cleansing and purifying, it is often used for clearing unwanted energies and promoting spiritual growth.

TOURMALINE

Protects against negative energies and promotes grounding stability.

Its

TIGERS EYE

Is it a good grounding stone, and is it associated with strength and courage?

CLEAR QUARTZ

It is what is called a master gem; it can be placed alongside other gems to enhance its abilities. When all else fails and you cannot get hold of any other crystal, the powerful, clear quartz will work just as well. It is one of the most powerful healing gems to have around.

Crystals are often used in many practices like Reiki, sound healing, meditation retreats, yoga practices, and many more.

Not everyone uses crystals on their spiritual journey, and that's ok. I do, however, like to fill my home with natural materials, and crystals have always been a good healing gem for me, particularly clear quartz, so don't feel like just because you have a spiritual awakening, you have to surround yourself with all these items, because that's not what spirituality is about. What I write here is from personal experiences and what helped me on my path; yours may be different from mine.

Understanding the masculine and feminine energies.

You may wonder what the masculine and feminine energies have to do with finding your power within. Well, let me explain about these energies. So, we all have masculine and feminine energy. It doesn't have anything to do with sexuality, processing feminine or masculine energies. We have both masculine and feminine energy within us. Most females today have suppressed their feminine energy, and so have a lot of males, but first, let's go a bit deeper into the meaning of these energies.

Masculine energy is often associated with traits like strength, ambition, focus, reason, and logic. Also associated with action, taking charge, and leadership.

Positive traits: ambition, courage, assertiveness, clarity, focus and will

Negative traits include being overly aggressive and controlling.

The feminine energy is intuitive, creative, fiery, passionate, empathetic, patient, and nurturing.

When out of balance, you can feel more friction and stress.

Today, many women, especially, are suppressing their feminine energy for many reasons like trauma, abuse, shame, and broken relationships. This causes them to step into the masculine energy; most often, we don't realise this until we do deep inner work. In cases like abuse, we put up an armor of protection because we think it's a way of being strong, hence the masculine trait. We get used to this and go about our daily lives not realizing it.,

Another big example is that feminine energy, also known as fire energy, is also passionate energy, and for a woman to carry this energy often feels shameful because other females are threatened by this energy, because they think the woman should not show that kind of energy. So, we feel ashamed of it.

Men also suppress feminine energy because they feel like it's a sign of weakness or because of their upbringing that men aren't supposed to cry.

The problem is how you are supposed to create something wonderful if you suppress your feminine energy. How are you supposed to nurture properly, and how can you have empathy for others? How can you find strength and focus on a task properly if your masculine energy is suppressed?

To balance the feminine energy, start by practicing self-care and self-love. Get creative, move your body and dance. Wear clothes that make you feel good. Do your hair up. Embrace your creative flow. Heal inner child wounds so you can fully become the powerful woman you're meant to be. Set a day where you can just flow with life; don't plan anything; let your intuition guide you. Listen to what feels good.

To balance the masculine energy, cultivate a positive mindset, act, and focus on what makes you happy.

Notice the traits within yourself. Once balanced, you get a sense of harmony and fulfilment.

The more inner work you do, the more understanding you have of yourself. Everything I write in this book is everything I discovered within myself. Of course, your journey will be different from mine, and sometimes what works for one doesn't necessarily work for the other. I had to go through a ton of different practices to find what was right for me. Take meditating, for example; I find focus meditation works better for me, like crafting, colouring, drawing, and writing, because I can't meditate in pure silence. I also found that further down my spiritual journey, it wasn't about sitting in the lotus position and yoga practices as most spiritual people do. Don't get me wrong, I'm not judging. I think that's great, but for me, it's about stillness, living in the present moment, enjoying every bit with love in your heart, and helping those around you while maintaining your inner peace. It's about creating a life you have always wanted, which you can do. Lives for living, we haven't come here to suffer.

As you can see, the first half of this book is about doing inner work for your healing journey, and although healing is an ongoing process, it gets much easier and becomes more enjoyable because you are finding so much out about yourself that you want to know more and once you have got past that loop you're on your way to being the master of your own reality.

Now that you have cleared so much of the unwanted crap that you have been carrying for most of your life, you make room for more new, healthy stuff.

The next part of this book is where the fun and magic begin as I take you on a journey to finding your purpose and stepping into your power with confidence, provided you follow the steps and continue to do the inner work. You will succeed.

You will start to recognise your gifts and talents and the ability to read the language of the universe, and the more you practice, the more you will develop. Even so, understand that it isn't always about tapping into your gifts, but it's about returning to yourself, the love and light being that you are.

The self-discovery path

Who am I?

What is my purpose?

There's got to be more to life than this.

These were the questions I regularly asked myself. The questions are good!! And how often do people ask questions about themselves? Not very often, as we are too focused on the outside world. This is the first step to discovering who you are and your purpose. You know when you're on the path to recovery when you start to get inquisitive with good, healthy questions. This is the huge shift in the mindset when you're getting to know yourself on deeper levels. You're finally out of the loop; you have freed up some space in your mind to explore! From here, it's like you have been given the key to let yourself out of the prison shell that you created in your mind, and you're seeing the world for the first time. Your brain is on the go! There's no stopping you now. You feel freer to explore your mind, body, and soul and the world around you. At times, you may relapse into the darkness, but that is ok because, from your inner work, you know that this situation is trying to tell you something, so instead of going into victim mode, you are in the mindset of working through it and seeing the lesson it is presenting you, you want to know more and more about yourself, so you set on a mission to find your passions, what makes you thrive, what's your purpose, it just means that some else is waiting to be dealt with but the good news is, shadow work gets easier and less uncomfortable and less painful. I couldn't get enough of all the questions; some days, I used to overwhelm myself with the number of questions I asked. Why do I always do that when I'm cooking? Do I really need to get up at 7.30 in the morning? Loads and loads of questions, some seem relevant, don't they? Well, not to me. How can we evolve if we don't ask the questions?

I had only ever been a single mum working the odd cleaning job while suffering from depression. I had no hobbies, only listening to music, as it was music that got me through some difficult situations. The truth is, I never wanted to be here back then. If I went on a date, the question I always got was, "What do you do for a living?" or "What do you do in your spare time when you are not a mother?" What could I say? "Oh, I suffer from depression, and I am as boring as they come because I don't leave the house, and when I'm not crying, I'm listening to sad music." No wonder I was single. Something had to change, so that's when I started searching for what I love to do! I first started doing courses; I had an interest in psychology and counselling, and in four courses, I passed CBT and advanced CBT, followed by psychology and counselling and body language. I had already done levels 1 and 2 in counselling a while ago.

I then went on to crafting, making gemstone jewellery, candles and bookbinding journals, which I opened a little Etsy shop. At this point, I couldn't stop!! I went into herbalism and natural medicine and loved it. I still study to this day, five years on. I started writing books and got into coaching as I have a gift for helping people. Then I went into Reiki and, after two attunements, became a Reiki practitioner heading for my third attunement for a master's level. The learning didn't end there; in fact, it became addictive!! I was bringing out so many gifts and talents that I didn't even know existed!! The more inner work I do, the more I find.

Then, I went on to ancestral healing and past regression hypnosis, which became an interesting subject. One of my personal favorites was the art of manifestation, which I started to teach. I also tapped into my physics and started to teach others how to tap into their own psychic powers. I had read over 30 books during my awakening and wrote five myself. I took qigong and learnt about the meridians in the body and sound healing. My passion so far is focused on healing the mind, body, and soul. I then went on to learn about the chakra system. Learning about quantum physics and quantum jumping, light activation, and raising consciousness. It was not bad coming from someone who believed they could only do cleaning jobs. We don't realise how much we are capable of.

I was still unsure of my purpose; all I knew was that I help people; at this moment in time, it's all about me. I don't mean that in any selfish way because I will still help people in need, but what I mean is my focus is always on my inner work; it's never on the outside, and the outside world is irrelevant to me. I find that the light I created within is enough to help others. I just maintain that light, and others follow in pursuit. The self-discovery path never ends because you're always finding out more about yourself, and it's the same with the healing journey; there is always something to heal; after all, there are passed-down ancestral patterns. I thought that the inner journey was a temporary one, but it isn't; it's lifelong!

Chasing dopamine's

Serotonin and dopamine are both brain chemicals that affect the mood. Dopamine's contributes to feelings of pleasure, motivation, and satisfaction; they are the feel-good chemicals that are released when something is pleasurable and enjoyable, like buying something new, eating something nice, or listening to good music. The serotonin chemical contributes to feelings of happiness, feelings of calm, well-being and stability. They are triggered by daily activities like going for walks in nature, getting a decent night's sleep, etc. They help regulate mood, body temperature, and appetite.

Both chemicals are vital for growth, metabolism sleep. Low levels of serotonin play a role in depression and anxiety. High levels can cause physical and psychological symptoms.

Humans naturally chase and crave dopamine, but the problem is that they crave the instant dopamine release, like eating tasty junk foods, spending excessive amounts of money and drinking lots of alcohol, scrolling through Facebook, watching videos, etc., and we get hooked on these unhealthy habits. This makes it hard to chase one's dream as it takes time for the dopamine to release.

One of the most effective ways to remove unhealthy habits and still have your healthy dopamine fix is to walk in nature. Remove yourself from unhealthy habits like phones, TV, and any other habit because when you walk in nature, it instantly releases feel-good chemicals. Because we live in a society where people are chasing money, love, happiness, and material things, they no longer appreciate the small things around them, and we take them for granted. The reason why those who are awakening is that appreciating the beauty around us and being grateful for the small things allows us to release our feel-good chemicals and still work on our goals and dreams. We can do this because we have swapped our unhealthy fixes for healthy fixes.

Everything I write in this book is to help you find the power within, but you cannot do that until you understand what stops you from accessing your inner power. Which is why I thought it would be important to write about serotonin and dopamine.

I found this all out when I was breaking generational patterns. I had an overspending habit and a huge love for food but mostly junk food. No matter how much I tried to save or diet, nothing would work. I tried spell work and manifestation, but nothing worked. I realised that a lot of people are just like that, scrolling on Facebook, hooked on junk food, and spending money. So, I looked deeper into it and came across the article on serotonin and dopamine. Of course, that is why spiritual people do what they do; we are not weird or crazy for hugging a tree. In fact, we know exactly what we are doing.

To achieve your goals and chase your dreams, we need an alternative dopamine fix! Here are some ways to release the feel-good chemical in a healthy way

Nature… get in touch with all your senses and really appreciate the beauty around you. Noticing the beautiful birds and butterflies. If the weather is bad, then notice the calmness of the rain and the softness of the snow.

Stop complaining

I once took a walk in nature, and it was so windy that my hair was blowing all over the place. Before my spiritual awakening, I would have been annoyed at that. Instead, I loved the feel of the wind blowing through my hair. A lady walked past me and said, "This weather is awful in summer." I said, "I love it." She looked at me as if to say, weird lady! See why we get classed as weird. Don't get me wrong, there's nothing wrong with looking forward to something good, but when you find happiness, beauty, and excitement in the here and now, in the small things, you unlock the love and happiness within. That is your answer for releasing your feel-good chemicals in a healthy way, allowing you to chase your dreams because you have no need to crave more feel-good chemicals, because they are being naturally released within you.

Try it!! Look for the beauty now in whatever you're doing, grab a cup of your favorite drink, sit down and sip it mindfully, really notice how good it tastes, notice the smell, look at the beauty in your cup, what is the design? When you go about your day in the present moment, being mindful, you start to see beauty everywhere.

Do more of what you love to do

Whether that be reading, playing the guitar, or getting creative

Eating food that helps release dopamine, like fish, eggs, milk, cheese, yogurt, nuts, seeds, avocados, and bananas

Exercise for 20 minutes a day to boost your mood

Getting enough sleep

Listening to music

Reduce saturated fats and pay attention to gut health

Breathwork to reduce stress

We all have psychic abilities.

From as far back as I can remember, I have always had the ability to just know things and sense things. I was very good at reading people and would often give insight into their future. I was the weird kid, as they call it. I wasn't interested in the typical kiddy stuff or even teenage stuff for that matter, heck, I don't even bother with the typical adult stuff, not what's classed as normal anyway, but eventually, the bullying got worse, and I knew I needed to try and fit in. It wasn't long before that was a disaster after developing more personalities in the hope of finding one that would be liked by others. It was exhausting!!

Anyway, back to psychic abilities.

So yes, we are all born with them, but we often switch them off or try to dismiss them, or if you're like someone who has the gift of clairaudience (clear hearing) and a history of schizophrenia, you fear them!! My gifts were screaming at me from day one; I could not switch them off. Fear was getting the better of me; I could have quite easily manifested schizophrenia. It's important to understand what psychic abilities are and how they tie into everything I wrote about so far.

Let's first talk about the " clairs," what they are, how to tap into them, and how they go hand in hand with manifesting and following the universe's language.

Clairvoyance (clear vision) is probably the most common one that you have heard the most. A clairvoyant often sees their visions in their mind's eyes, a bit like watching a TV screen in their head. It is perceived through the 3rd eye's chakra. Messages are received visually and not necessarily as words or songs. When it comes to clairvoyance, spirits/souls send messages into the mind's eye in the form of an image or a scene that plays out while you watch.

Clairaudients (clear hearing) are the ability to hear other dimensions and frequencies of the spirit world. Clairaudient can come through in many ways and can be different for everyone. It may be through spoken words, song lyrics, or ringing in the ears. People with clairaudience often have a passion for music, and certain songs may stand out to them as they have a specific meaning. They often talk to themselves or out loud. Coming up with ideas, going through scenarios, and asking questions about life. Internal chatter can also have another meaning; you could be guided by your soul or higher self without even realizing it; keep listening. People with clairaudience often get thoughts and ideas that just come out of the blue!! They can often telepathically communicate by reading other people's thoughts.

Clairsentience (clear feel): clairsentients receive their messages through physical sensations and feelings in their body. They are good at feeling subtle energies in others. They may feel warmth, cold spots, tightness, and pressure in their bodies to interpret their messages. They can feel sudden emotions like happiness, sadness, anger, and anxiety from others. They can also pick up on subtle body language and facial expressions.

Claircognizance (clear knowing): someone with claircognizance will receive their messages through a sudden intuitive "knowing" or understanding without any clear explanation or clear reason. They just know almost as if the information was downloaded directly into their mind without needing to see, hear, or feel it physically. It's a clear understanding without the need for sensory input. Some believe that claircognizance is a result of connecting with a higher power or spirit guides, or ancestors who pass information directly through the mind.

Now you have a little understanding of the clairs, let's see which is your most dominant Clair. If you close your eyes and imagine you're on a deck chair in front of the sea, you are looking at the warm sun shining down on your face. You feel the sand slipping between your toes, and the waves are crashing in front of you. You turn to your right, and you see two people playing volleyball; you notice the smile on their faces, the colour of their hair, and the clothes they are wearing. Now, open your eyes. If you could feel the warmth of the sun on your face and the sand beneath your toes as though it were real, then Clairsentient is your most dominant Clair. If you can hear the waves crashing in the sea quite loudly, then your clairaudient is your most dominant Clair. If you see every detail of the two playing volleyball down to features on the face and what they were wearing in detail, then clairvoyance is your most dominant Clair. Claircognizance is an overall sense of just knowing things. Or you could possess all the claims. Now that you have found your most dominant Clair, you can work on expanding your gifts, but first, let's go into the importance of tapping into your gifts.

Tapping into your psychic abilities is not just for reading other people's futures, but it's for you to navigate through life. It can help you to spot risky situations, resolve dilemmas, seek self-improvement, and spot predators. It also goes hand in hand with following the universe's language, as spoken about earlier, as this opens your mind and heart to receive and hear the messages. There are many exercises you can use to strengthen your psychic abilities, and the most common exercise is meditation, connecting to nature, and tapping into all your senses. Keeping dream journals is also a great idea, as messages are always in the dream world. I will soon be writing a book on tapping into your psychic power.

The art of manifestation

This is where most of the magic begins!!

Coming across this article was one of the best things that ever happened to me on my spiritual path. Understand that everyone's path is different, and you may be guided onto a completely different path, but most people I know who are like-minded will inevitably come across manifestation and the chakras that I will get onto next. The reason is that we are manifesting all the time, good or bad; we are making reality happen, even the bad shit! No other people are responsible for our lives; we are. I hear it all the time when someone says, "It's his fault my life turned out like this!! Remember, there are always choices. It's a gift that we all have, and once you free yourself from the limitations of the mind, the more you become a master at manifesting. But first, you need to foster a positive mindset, which is why I talked about rewiring the brain and the power of positive mantras and affirmations.

Although manifestation was something I picked up on at the beginning of my spiritual journey, it wasn't something I was passionate about at the time. I didn't realise that I was already doing it, and I sure didn't realise how important it would be in my life until a few years ago.

Manifestation is the ability to make your dreams happen with the power of thought and intention. Of course, you must take the action steps.

The first thing you need to do is be sick with what it is that you want to manifest. Believe it or not, this is not as easy as you think it is for most people. Operate from their brains, not from their hearts. I would eat most of the dreams that were rooted within our hearts. Burned away for reasons like, "It's silly to think I can't do that, or maybe one day, but not now." I need to be realistic.

We must be in line with what our hearts truly want, and not what we think we want. Anybody can write a list of what they want. But when you really dig deep inside your heart, it ends up different from what's inside your head; it's not easy, most people's hearts are closed off.

To do this, spend a few days asking yourself some deep questions, and don't be afraid to dream big. The next step to manifest is to visualise as many times as possible a day. So, if you want a new home, you rarely see what your home looks like. What does the wallpaper look like? What does the furniture look like? How big is the garden? How many bedrooms does it have? Is there a shop or a field nearby? You need to put as much detail as you can into it.

Set up a vision board with pictures of your dream home and place it where you can see it. Place much detail on the vision board. The next step would be to take inspired action, and this can look like saving money or taking up a new career with better pay. Along with the action steps, you need to act like you already have your dream home. So, treat your home as though it's your new home. Be grateful for what you already have so you can make room for more. Then, you will need to believe. This is not easy, but it's vital. You must trust that it's on its way. And finally, surrender. Try not to attach yourself to the outcome. Life is about the journey and not the destination. When you attach yourself to the outcome, you block the ability to manifest. You miss opportunities that come your way. You miss the messages in the synchronicities that are all around you when you align with them.

The universe sends you on a path that your hearts must follow. We also must keep up an appearance to fit in, so we don't feel stupid about manifesting. We must be in line with what we truly want. And not what we think we want. Anybody can write a list of what they want. But when you really dig deep inside your heart for what you really want, it's not easy. Most people's hearts are closed off.

We must be aligned with what our hearts truly want, and not what we think we want. Anybody can write a list off the top of their heads if they want, but knowing what's inside your heart is not easy, especially if your heart is closed off.

When I feel, myself getting attached to the outcome, I feel stagnant. I no longer get opportunities for inspiration, and I feel stuck. The everyday mundane world gets stressful. So, I say, you know what I want? To surrender, I take myself to nature and I simply be with nature itself. I then journal like I write a letter to the university. I surrender, and I will focus. On me for a while. Like self-love, I soon gained my trust back in the universe just by bringing it.

Although healing is lifelong, and what I mean by that is that not just the mind heals, but the body and soul, as well as ancestral healing, which I will explain later, the biggest part of healing has taken place and has now left room for new beginnings. I came across the subject of manifesting and was inquisitive to know more about it. After 4 years, I became pretty good at manifesting!!

So, you probably wonder what the word manifest means. Well, it's like this. We manifest all the time, good or bad, into our lives, and you're probably wondering why on earth I would want to manifest bad things, right? Unless you're aware of manifestation and how it is, then you won't even be aware that you are manifesting bad things because thoughts are taken for granted. So,

I'll get the point: manifesting is the ability to bring your thoughts into things by setting an intention to set a goal you want to achieve, then visualizing it, and then take action steps, believing it will happen, and trusting that the universe will deliver it. Most importantly, release the control of the outcome, and try not to attach yourself to the outcome, as it blocks the process. Instead, focus on the here and now and act like you already got what you wished for. This aligns your energy with the energy you set yourself up for, meaning if you want success, you've got to act successful and feel the success for it to come back to you.

To understand this concept is to know that there are many different versions of you in different timelines. There is already a successful you, a bad you, a rich you, and so on. You're all happening right now, but in different realities. Hard to believe, isn't it? It's not that hard once you learn the universe's language, as I call it. You just need to align with that frequency in the now because you already have what it is you asked for.

So, here's what you need to do.

What is your purpose?

What is your passion? What makes your heart sing? What drives you?

Most people operate from the head and not the heart; we make decisions based on what the head is telling us because it may seem realistic and ideal for this given time. It may be that deep down inside, you're too embarrassed to say what you really want out of fear of what others think. Maybe you cannot dream big because you think you are not good enough, so you dream small. Whatever the reason, you need to spend a few seconds asking what it is you truly want from your heart and not your head. If you are not aligned with your heart, then the manifestation will not run smoothly. This process took me over a year to figure out. In Fact, I did a lot of exploring different things, from arts and crafts to playing guitar, because all I ever knew was being a single mum, my only hobby was listening to music. I went down the self-discovery path, tapping into my gifts and talents before I found my true purpose. I knew I was meant to be helping others, but I didn't know what way. Being clear on your purpose is the main important part.

Set your first goal

Once you have established your purpose and found what your heart truly desires, then you can set your first goal; it's a good idea to start off small when setting a goal, so you don't get too overwhelmed and lose your focus, because you will need to maintain focus at all times.

It helps to use a vision board or somewhere where you can see your goals and plan of action. This will help you to stay focused on your goal at hand. And each time you make progress towards your goals, you can monitor your accomplishments. This will give you more initiative to keep moving forward. Vision boards don't have to be fancy; they can just be a part of your wall where you can stick notes up so you can see your achievements and accomplishments. And if you like, you can even get creative and stick up some pictures of your dream holidays or dream house, etc.

Visualization

Once your goal is set, the next step is to visualize. For example, e.g. if your goal is to move house, you will need to put as much vision as you can into your visualization. What does the house look like? How big is it? What does the decor look like? Are there shops nearby? Are there Neighbours? Bring in all your senses and smell the flowers in the garden. What do you hear? Really go into depth. The brain does know the difference between belief and reality. This is what it means to think things into reality; thoughts become things. Place pictures of your ideal house on your vision board. Spend 10 minutes every day visualizing your dreams and then build up from there.

Take action

Whether that be ringing around houses or even going to look at houses, do you need to save money first? Or filling out forms. Whatever that is, take small, inspiring actions towards your goal. Don't forget to praise and celebrate your achievements on your vision board.

Practice gratitude

By being thankful for what you already have, you leave room to invite more. Make a list of how many things you are grateful for, including all the small things like the sun shining.

Raise your vibrations

This doesn't mean that you must always be happy and positive, as that is unrealistic and not healthy. Instead, it's about not attaching yourself too much to negative circumstances. Feel the emotions, make sense of them, and find solutions to work through them rather than attaching yourself to the emotions and dwelling on them. Low vibrations are things like negativity, gossip, complaining, greed, anger, illness, and hate. While high vibration, I love compassion, positivity, laughter, and joy. When I speak in the terms of the universe language, what I mean is energy! What you give out, you will attract back. So, if you operate in gossip, you will attract drama. If you vibrate in negativity, you will attract negative situations. You attract what you vibrate at. So, you want to be vibrating from higher vibrations to attract those things.

Surrender

I spoke a little about surrender and how it works previously. You must get to a place where you are not controlling the outcome. If you attach yourself to the outcome, you will miss the opportunities and inspiration that come in the present moment, and manifestation will be slow, or it just won't happen. You need to enjoy the moment! And let the universe do the rest.

Believe and trust

This part is also important because it requires you to believe you already have it! Let go of any doubts and fears holding you back and trust in the process. It's all about consciousness and remember you are a multidimensional being; there is already a successful you, a happy, peaceful you, and there are many Yous. You are literally creating your own reality. You are becoming that person, aligning yourself with the power of thought and matching the vibration. After all, everything is energy and vibrating, including your thoughts.

Now, I've given you the steps you're probably thinking. It sounds easy!! Well, that depends on many factors as to how quickly manifestation happens. So, let's look at a few obstacles that may slow down the process.

Fear

I put fear at the top of the list because it's the most common one, and it was one that drove me crazy for quite a while. Fear of failure, fear of not being good enough, fear of rejection, fear of stepping out of the comfort zone, fear of the unknown, yes, we humans do not like stepping into the unknown. You must get to the bottom of your fears and understand that you are not your emotions. You are a spiritual being living a human existence. You are the creator of your own reality. Feel the fear and do it anyway; what do you have to lose?

Imposter syndrome

Yes, I have that too!! Imposter syndrome is when you feel like a fraud; you feel that you don't deserve your awards and certificates for your accomplishments. You feel like you always need to know more when you know enough. Imposter syndrome often comes from trauma and past abuse, being told you're not good enough.

Finances

Try cultivating a positive mindset around money by being mindful of your words. By saying things like "I'm always poor," the universe just hears the word "poor." Remember that the universe speaks in terms of energy, and that is the energy you're putting out. It's a "lack of" energy.

Practice positive affirmation and speak in present terms like "I already have money." Remember that you are bringing that existence to you. You already have it; you just need to align with that "you" that you are creating.

Practice gratitude and be grateful for what you already have. Remember that greed is a low vibrational frequency, and manifestations work better from a high vibrational frequency.

Identify your challenges and make constructive steps towards reducing them.

Declutter your physical space and remove any negative associations around money so you can make room for abundance.

Shift your mindset. What are the limited beliefs that you tell yourself about money that might be holding you back?

Maintain a positive outlook and believe it's on its way.

Seek support if needed

Be patient, as manifesting takes time and effort.

The belief system

Understanding their belief system. I wrote previously about the belief system.

Their belief system is the stories we tell ourselves that we believe to be true, and we tend to stay rigid in that belief without evidence to back it up. I have learned on my journey that it's very important to keep an open mind when exploring different possibilities. Sometimes, a man cannot comprehend certain things, so we booked if we place it to one side, speaking from the ego mind, that's not true. I believe this, et cetera. It's OK that you cannot comprehend something because, at that moment, you're not meant to. But staying open-minded allows the truth to come in at some point. Remember, I'm referring to your truth.

I have changed my belief system many times because new knowledge comes to me that brings me new insight to change my perception of how I look at situations and people. When we delve deep into the belief system, the stories can come from our parents, friends, schools and even be passed down from ancestors. For example, my father told me I wasn't clever enough to do a psychology course. It shattered my dreams at the time because we most often believe what our parents say, but I went along and did it anyway and was surprised at how well I did, but that wasn't enough evidence for me because my father's words lay rooted within me.

I was always at the bottom of the class and never took any exams because I didn't see the point; I would fail anyway. That was my story that I told myself. I was often told I was dumb, three sheets to the wind were another saying I heard a lot. All these were stuck within and woven into our belief system. So, we go about our lives, settling for what we think we can do. For me, it was cleaning jobs, because I believe I couldn't do anything else.

Let's look at some familiar stories. We bring into the belief system.

I'm not good enough.

I'm too old to do that.

I'm not clever enough.

I'm not worthy enough.

I did that, I failed, so I can't do it again.

When we sit down and take the time to question these stupid, meaningful stories we tell ourselves, we actually realise it's not true. But then we create another story, like OK. I am clever enough, but the timing is not right. What we need to do is to get to the root of why we think like this. We can change our belief system at any given time. And when we do watch out, the shift happens, and our opportunities flood black ripples.

What are the stories you tell yourself? Are they true? Are you too old?

This is why shadow work helps. The more inner work you do, the quicker the manifestation will

I feel you, fear

I understand you

Walk with me if you must

But I'm doing this with or without you

Angel numbers

Angel numbers are repeated numbers or pattern sequences that are interpreted as messages sent to us from the divine or a higher power. These numbers or sequences appear all the time, but we don't take any notice due to our hectic lifestyles. They can present themself as numbers like 111, 222, 444, or even 23, 32, and so on.

Each number has a specific meaning, offering guidance and insight on our spiritual path. It can be anything from career, personal growth and relationships. They are often seen on clocks, phones, or car number plates, but can appear on anything.

Angel number 1 or 111, 1111 often represents spiritual growth, guidance, and support, but it can also represent twin flames, as the number 11 can mean infinity.

Angel number 444 means that you are protected. 333 is creativity, and 222 can be balance, love, and harmony.

Angel numbers often become apparent at the start of your spiritual awakening but can be seen as a coincidence. The further along your journey, you start to see that there are too many to be just coincidences; it's as though you are literally having a conversation with the divine.

Try for yourself now.

Ask a question, but also ask, but don't ask a question that needs a yes or no answer. Ask something like, "What will the next 2 weeks hold for me?" Be patient while waiting for your answer, as it can come instantly or can take a couple of days, depending on how much you are listening to them.

If you are always stuck in your head, then you want to hear or see the message. It is only in the present moment that you will see them. It would be beneficial to be mindful of everything you do so you don't miss the message. It does get easier in time with practice.

If you see repeated numbers or sequences, Google the meaning, and it will explain several meanings, and your intuition will pick up the right one for you.

I believe that we all have guardian angels who are looking out for us and guiding us on our way. I know I do.

Understanding synchronicities

Synchronicities are incidents that occur at just the right time. They can appear as messages, quotes, song lyrics, spoken words, in people in shop windows, in pictures in the clouds, in symbols, and even in animals holding messages. They align perfectly when you are on the right path and flowing smoothly. Most often, people put these down to coincidence, and I used to be one of those people until I learnt that there is no such thing as coincidence! It's as though the universe is communicating with you. You're doing the pots, and you're thinking of something when a song comes on with lyrics that answer your question; you realise this further down the spiritual path. People show up at just the right time, for e.g., I knew my purpose was to be a Reiki healer, but I had very little money and had to save. I enquired and found one near me who was willing to give me Reiki sessions in return for some Reiki symbol drawings. I am now attuned to Reiki.

You must actively pay attention to the coincidental events that are going on around you to follow the synchronicities, and that means stepping out of your head. These events will have deeper meanings personal to you. Interpreting them as guidance and following them with an open mind. By doing this, you're taking action that is aligned with your intuition and inner knowing when the synchronicities happen. What you're doing is noticing patterns in your life and using them to help you make decisions and your next move. In time, this becomes like a second language, the language of the universe.

By consciously paying attention to your surroundings and the people who enter your life, you will start to notice patterns, symbols, numbers, and themes. When these had significance to me, I would look up the meaning to see if it resonated with me. I also kept a dream journal, as often these patterns would show up in my dreams. Trust your intuition when the synchronicities appear and take the time to pause and reflect on how you feel; often, you get nudges as though something is telling you something, that is your intuition speaking.

Stay open-minded and don't dismiss the coincidences as there is no such thing. Instead, consider what the messages hold for you. Write down your experiences to help you analyze any patterns and to help you understand the message more. Consider how the synchronicities might relate to your current life, goals, challenges, and emotional well-being, then take action to explore further.

It's important to practice mindfulness and be in the present moment to enhance your ability to notice synchronicities. Avoid analyzing, as this can become overwhelming and confuse you. Be patient because sometimes the full message can be clearer in time.

I often come across people who are like angels in disguise because they serve as messengers bringing positive affirmations and words of comfort at just the right time and often serve as a message that you're on the right path or need to take a different path. Synchronicities happen in the external world, and it's your inner world where you decipher them from. I always find that tapping into your psychic abilities helps with this, which I will go into later in this book.

The world is full of chaos and sadness,

Create your own world

Forget about that madness.

Don't live your life in fear and sorrow,

Live your life like there's no tomorrow.

Shine so bright, just like the stars,

Be your authentic self,

That is who you are.

Doesn't matter if you're a little weird,

Just be happy, wipe your tears.

Listen to your heart and do what's best,

Because life is too short for anything less.

What does it mean to surrender?

One of the most profound experiences on my spiritual journey was reading "The Surrender Experiment" by Michael Singer. A book that completely turned my life around! I won't go too much into what it's about in case you haven't read it, but it's about letting go of control. For me, this ties into the synchronicities I spoke about in the last chapter. To be able to surrender, you must put your complete trust and faith into the universe and trust that whatever happens is all for your higher good, even if it feels uncomfortable at the moment. By continuing to do your inner work and not focusing on the outside world, there is only you and the universe talking. Of course, you may have children and partners to attend to, but to me, they are part of your inner world.

It's not easy to surrender, to give up trying to control life, as it's a human's natural habit to control. Often, this comes down to fear of the unknown; let's face it, who wants to step into the unknown, not knowing what's going to happen next? In my experience, this takes a lot of inner work, healing, and faith in your inner wisdom to do this. As I mentioned before that fear was at the top of my list of the obstacles that we face because we fear so many things, but we don't realise that fear is just an illusion. One of my quotes that helped me through the fear was, "I feel your fear, I understand you, but I'm doing this with or without you." I came to realise at the time that a certain amount of anxiety is normal and it's normal to feel it when put in situations out of our comfort zone. By repeating those words, I was allowing myself to feel without letting the emotions take over. After all, you are not your emotions; you're much more. Find whatever mantra you want that helps you through it. Once we realise that fear comes from the ego, we start to see the ego for what it is; we step away from the ego and see ourselves from a different perspective.

Whenever things got tough for me, and I felt like I was in control, I would take myself to nature, look up to the sky, and I would say I surrender, then take some powerful, deep, slow breaths and bring myself to the present moment. I would notice the birds, the sunshine, the trees and flowers, and the different colours. I would notice how I felt, and most often, I felt calm, relaxed, and at peace. I would then say a prayer to the universe about how I feel and then leave everything into the universe's hands and trust what comes next. I would then thank the universe with a smile on my face, knowing that everything was going to be ok. It's not long after that floods of inspirations opportunities come flooding, and I'm put back onto the flow of the universe where synchronicities come again.

The reason this happens is that we block the connection by low vibrational states, like stress or illness. Keeping yourself well-grounded daily helps, and to do this, you can use visualization meditations; these are guided meditations, and they can be found on YouTube, you visualize that you have roots growing from you. There are many different meditation techniques to choose from. I also learnt that the importance of raising your vibrations will help keep you connected with the universe.

It was reading the surrender experiment book that completely transformed my life! I felt the shift instantly! Ever since then, I've been consistent in my writing, and I'm now sailing through writing my books. I've managed to keep my overspending and overeating at bay; I feel more at peace. I can relax more as I literally watch my life unfold right in front of my eyes. As Michael says in his book, it really is as though the universe is handing you the steppingstones, and all you must do is step on them.

The voice of the universe

I see you

I see you shine

Can you see me

Can you see my sign

I hear you

I hear your voice

Can you hear me

Your words, I rejoice.

I feel you

I feel your love

Do you feel me

Close by you and above

I hold you

I hold you tight

I surround you with love.

And fill you with light.

Do you believe in me?

As I believe in you

I've got your back

You got mine, too

I trust you

I hope you trust me

For I am you

Can't you see

When the universe steps in

I was eating a sandwich one day when all a sudden I couldn't swallow, and I put the sandwich down and didn't eat anything for the rest of the day.

The following morning, I got to have my breakfast, and again, I couldn't swallow. It was as though food was getting stuck in my throat. This continued for a few days until I couldn't even eat soup.

I ended up in bed poorly, and eventually, I rang the hospital as I was experiencing shortness of breath and palpitations. The hospital sent an ambulance as they were concerned that it would be my heart, but after all the tests, they found nothing, so I came home.

I continued to stay in bed, and by this point, I was lacking energy due to over a week with no food. I had the ambulance the second time as I was convinced there was something seriously wrong, but nothing was found again, so they sent me home.

I ended up going to Chesterfield, 75 miles away from home, to stay with my family.

I had temporary doctors who did all the tests they could possibly think of, only to find nothing again, so they admitted me to the hospital to have a camera down my throat. This had a little waiting list of two weeks, but I had already gone two weeks with no food.

Every time I tried to eat, I would experience pain in my esophagus at this point. I was convinced I had cancer.

I lay down and started to meditate. I had never meditated so much in my life. I was so full of fear about being visited by monks and angels. It was a beautiful experience, and I just kept going back to visit this place until my time was up. But then I heard a voice that told me to sit up and sip the soup.

After a month of no food and being totally bed-bound, I was admitted to the hospital again and placed on drips. They did every test they called and still didn't find anything, although I was still waiting for the camera to be down my throat. With the trips, I started to pick up and could manage to go to the toilet. And I thought I was getting better, but I was wrong. Every time I died, it was the scariest thing I've ever gone through. Then, I had a sense of calm wash over me. I was, I did. I started it with the soup and drinking water.

Before my very eyes, I had a flash vision of a lady holding clear quartz in her hand and

knew I had to buy one. My angel guide told me to use my hands to heal my tummy. After that, I placed my hands on my tummy. She said, imagine you healing yourself. So, I did, and I did this all the time for a few days. Then, my clear quartz arrived. I always held the gem in my hand, and when I slept, I placed a clear quartz at the side of me. The morning after I woke, I was dancing in the kitchen to music. I went from bedbound to dancing. I don't know where this energy came from.

I had my camera down my throat. Done and waited a few days for the results. The results show a very small I act as an attorney, but they said that there was no way I would have got those symptoms from something so small. I was so happy that it wasn't something serious. It did take seven months to regain my appetite, but something magical happened. It was tough. I was given a new body, one that knew exactly what it wanted before I knew it. I was drinking herbal teas and eating healthy foods that I would have never eaten before, like avocados. No, no coffee, whole meal bread, rice and pasta, nuts and seeds. My body had taken a mind of its own.

The only thing I could not eat was fish because I could not swallow, and my body rejected it. But because I felt so healthy, I made the conscious decision to be a vegetarian and haven't touched me. Ever since. After an awful lot of journaling and hundreds of questions about what that was all about, I got to the bottom of it all. Crystal does have healing properties, and so do we. We had the ability to heal ourselves, and that food is medicine.

As you can see, sometimes the universe throws in some terrible life events that at the time are upsetting and even devastating, but there's always a reason behind it, and it is not always what it appears to be. Somewhere amongst the heartache is a plan for your higher good, but because you're living the awful experience, you don't see it. I know this now, so I know that whatever happens in my life, I can see the bigger picture the universe is presenting for me.

This all had to happen to me to discover all this. The universe made this happen. It was a huge wake-up call, and this led me because I could not eat. I am thinking about learning about Reiki. And studying foods, foods for detoxing, foods for boosting the immune system, etc.

I went down the holistic route for everything I started to have naturally. Ingredients for skincare and cleaning products. This just became a way of life for me. Although I still must work on my body, I feel much healthier. I don't eat sugar anymore, which is the main thing I wanted to cut out. There is one thing that I have learned: the healing journey is lifelong. It is something that becomes part of life.

I spent the next six months or so making natural skincare and cleaning products and exploring oils and essential oils. I documented everything that I made and the ingredients at the airport. I love to make herbal teas. In particular. Especially ritual tease that I can mindfully sit, with wise visualizing. The exploration is endless. Although. I spent a lot of time doing inner work, healing the mind, body and soul. I also help and teach others as I go along, sharing the knowledge and wisdom I find. I believe that this knowledge and wisdom should be available to everyone. Healing the body also became part of my everyday routine.

Sometimes, the universe steps in when we ignore the signs, and this is what happened to me. I had previously had to sort my diet out and take up exercise, and because I ignored the sign, I was put on the right track. I'm grateful for that because it worked out for my greater good, even though, at the time, I thought I was dying, and my world was falling apart.

Discovering your purpose

When I started asking the question of what my purpose is, I came across a comment that said If you want to know what your purpose is, look at your past because the breadcrumbs have been left for you. This couldn't be far from the truth.

I remember when I first met somebody who could heal; he didn't call it Reiki at the time. He is called the energy eagle. It was back when I was around 23 that I came across a guy who did tarot readings and claimed to be an energy healer.

Then the second time was during a course. I was doing health and social studies. The lady was a Reiki practitioner and ran courses on Reiki, and I remember her being drawn to me as I was very. Interested and inquisitive, even though he had no idea.

Then, I was told by two psychics that I had healing hands. Not to mention how my ex said my hands were like radiators.

Of course, these subtle signs go unnoticed because most of us are so busy dealing with the everyday stresses in life that we fail to see the signs. This is why I wrote this book, so you can quieten your mind and notice the signs and messages around you.

I knew at that moment what my purpose was, and with my knowledge of manifesting, I knew that once aligned with my true soul's purpose, the floodgates would start opening, and opportunities would come, and that was when I found a Reiki master and booked my first session.

On the phone call, my Reiki master told me a few things I will never forget. He said that I was psychic and that I'm a Reiki healer and always have been in my past lives. Well, that shiver down my spine happened again with a Deja-vu of a previous life I discovered during meditation, where I discovered I was a medicine woman and a healer.

So now, when I have the shiver, I know it's my soul talking to me, saying it's right what I'm thinking or saying.

I knew instantly. During my first Reiki session, my Reiki practitioner said I bet you used to read medical books. I said yes, I did. He said that I was like that, too. Not only can we spot where illnesses are, but we also intuitively pick up what they could be. Although Reiki healers. Do not diagnose.

The further I went into learning Reiki, the more I could see how everything happened for a reason and that it was all for this very day. That's it. I knew I had to be attuned, going back to the art and manifestation, when I spoke about what it was that I truly wanted, not from. Had but from the heart. Well, that was the first step into my manifestation, the alignment to my soul's purpose.

Manifestation started to happen faster than before, but I still had some obstacles to overcome, and fear was one of them. I often spent a lot of time in my comfort zone watching TV and scrolling down Facebook, overeating and overspending, and these were nasty little habits that I had to deal with to manifest quicker. I had to deal with these, but since finding my purpose, my focus shifted. Instead of focusing on my habits, I started to focus on what it was I wanted to do. I wanted to be a Reiki master, I wanted to be a successful author, and I wanted to teach. These are just a few of how. Because I have even bigger plans, I wake up each day, maintaining Focus on my dreams. And because my focus has shifted, I had no desire to overspend. Binge watching TV and overeating, which gets me to my second part of manifestation. Visualization.

Everything that I was doing from the start of my spiritual journey to now was removing obstacles, healing wounds and removing bad habits. I made my manifestation list in the beginning and didn't even realise. The only thing that changed on my list was that I wanted to be a counselor. Hence, the coaching. Most of it I was doing intuitively.

The step into manifestation was the action step, which was quite slow at first. I started writing my first book five years ago and stopped halfway through. And then went on to my second book and stopped three chapters in. Then, there was nothing for a long time. I often resorted to the sofa for a few weeks, which was rather frustrating. I didn't realise that when this happened, it was growth. It is happening and the mind. Body and soul need to rest.

While the transformation takes place, I found this out through journaling and meditation. Realised that I had to find balance. I was doing far too much in one go.

I had read many books on spiritual journeys, but the one that changed my life big time was A Surrender Experiment by Michael Singer. I won't give away too much for those who haven't read the book. He mastered the art of surrendering to the universe, stepping into the unknown, and trusting that the universe has your back. It is not just an easy thing to do, as we tend to naturally control our lives. This was. My next step, and I got it down to a tee. The idea is to focus on self-care like meditation, walks in nature and practicing living in the present moment. That is the present moment when you see the messages, inspiration, and opportunities. If you are not in the present moment, you miss these. Messages, inspiration, opportunities. The universe sends us people opportunities at just the right time, and when you're In Sync with the universe, it's as though you are given. The steppingstones, and all you must do is step on them. You live life with more peace, and you effortlessly watch it unfold in front of your eyes.

WHEN DESTINY CALLS

All the places we have lived

All the things that we did

All the people we knew

That left our path

Leaving the remains a few

They entered our lives

Bringing good and bad

To teach us lessons

We once had

The lessons we learn

Only makes us stronger

Some learn quick

And some take longer

For each day

Is a different day

What matters the most

I'd, we find our way

Please don't think

That you are worthless

You were put on this earth for a purpose

All the hurt

That you have beaten

Everything happens

For a reason

So, search for your path.

You will hear the call.

Walk as if you own it.

And you walk tall

Stay on your path

Your soul is calling

Continue forward

Without any stalling

Don't look behind

Keep going along

That's your destiny calling

That's where you belong

Michelle Marriott

The intelligence of the human body.

Did you know that the human body has a voice, too?

Yes, that's right!

A very intelligent vessel capable of healing itself and communicating through the senses.

Feelings of happiness, joy, warmth, peace and love can be an indicator of a spiritual state and connection.

Aches, pains, tingling and warmth

It can be interpreted as messages from the spirit.

Posture and facial expressions can be spiritual energy.

Intuition, gut feeling, or sudden insight can be spiritual communications through the body.

Our bodies also let us know when something is wrong and send us messages to rectify it.

I was going through a tough period where I was extremely sensitive to other people's energies as well as planetary changes like retrogrades, solar flares and moon cycles.

This tends to happen during a spiritual awakening, as there are so many changes going on in the mind and body.

The higher our consciousness goes, the more sensitive we become to things like food and energy. In turn, this can leave us depleted of energy ourselves. So, it's vital that we take care of ourselves.

I came across a post for a gong bath in my area and was curious to know more, so I went to the first one, and I was amazed at the results!

A gong bath, also known as sound healing, is a healing session using instruments such as gongs, singing bowls, chimes, rattles and chronic (a type of seashell), and you lie on a mat and relax and let the sound bathe around you.

A gong bath uses sound waves and vibrations to promote healing

You may feel sensations like tingly feelings on your skin or feel deep vibrations within your body. You may also feel hot and cold, and you may experience a lot of emotions coming up as sound healing releases unwanted energies that have been stored in your body.

You can also experience altered states of consciousness and may feel a sense of unity with everyone and everything, which is exactly what I experienced.

It was difficult in the first few sessions to relax, but I still reaped the benefits from the sessions. However, on the 3rd session, I went with stuck energy in my crown chakra as I was having pressure sensations there. So, the gong master placed me near the singing bowls; I'm guessing that was to release the stuck energy.

Halfway through the session, I saw a pink and white lotus flower open up at my crown chakra, and I felt a warmth energy showering out of my crown chakra and pouring down my body like a waterfall of energy that felt so serene; in fact, I cannot find the words to describe it.

Then my entire body went into pure stillness!! My mind and body were so relaxed that I had no aches, no pain, no jitters, no thoughts in my head, nothing, just pure stillness!! It was bliss, magical, it was like heaven on earth, that is the only way I can describe and yet those words don't even come close to the feeling I experienced.

When the session was over, I wanted to stay there; I didn't want to ever move from that spot, but when I came home the next few days, I was able to get back into that state.

A couple of months after that, I felt the shift into higher consciousness. I felt more love, more gratitude, more self-awareness, more peace, heightened intuition and was able to be more present, more mindful.

Then I started to connect with my body, feeling all these sensations, I had never felt before. It was as though all my chakras had individually developed their own voice! I could finally step out of my head and into my body and listen to all the messages my body had been trying to tell me all my life.

The gong baths had removed all the emotions that were stored in my lower chakras, allowing me to feel lighter and have more connection to what my body was communicating to me.

Some of the examples were

The sensation I had in the center of my chest that made me gasp for air was telling me to do breathwork; it wasn't that my heart was in as bad shape as I thought it was. So, when I started to do deep breathing, it stopped.

The stiffness in my neck was telling me that there was energy stuck, so I released it with a qigong session.

The headache at the back of my skull was telling me to meditate.

My bladder was telling me to slow down.

I started to ask my body if it was ok and what it wanted, and the funny thing was that I went to the shop and I asked my body what it wanted to eat, and as I walked across all the aisles, I heard " POISON POISON POISON" in my head so loud that I had to giggle! Everything in the shop was poisonous. I went to the fruit and veg section, and a voice said, decisively, "If I must," meaning that even the fruits and vegetables weren't quite right.

We take for granted that every little thing that happens to our bodies needs a doctor, but that is not always the case. The problem here is that we can manifest illnesses by placing too much focus on why our body is giving off these signals.

The more we listen to our bodies, the more we can prevent any future diseases.

Conscious living

I discovered what it meant to live consciously and how to find love, happiness and peace in the present moment. Although it took five years of practice, I'm certainly getting there. I did, however, must battle with my inner demons first to be able to tap into this beautiful, peaceful, harmonious space.

Below is a glimpse into my journal, where I had the pleasure of living a whole day in the present moment, and it was the best day of my life. Today, I spend most days in the present, although sometimes I can be caught off guard, but it is something I continue to work on.

Take a long, deep breath in and hold for five seconds. I'm slow. Open your eyes. What do you see? What do you hear? How do you feel?

```
It's Friday, 21st of the 2nd, 2025. The
time is 7:00 AM. I open my eyes and take a
deep breath, I tell myself, Today, I make a
conscious decision to be in the present
moment, and I will live consciously. I take
another deep breath, and I sit with my body
and For a few moments I asked my body, what
do you need right now? I hear a voice within
that says Reiki, and so I shall give my body
exactly just that. I place, a smile upon my
face and give myself permission to sit with
my body and heal it for half an hour,
knowing my body was in great hands.,
Literally. I told myself I would enjoy this.
```

I often tend to get bored while doing Reiki and I often quit after 10 minutes but this time, I was engrossed and so relaxed, that was telling myself to enjoy it, in fact, 30 minutes ,soon turned into an hour and a half, i enjoyed it that much.

I had to get out of bed as I had things to do. But then this quiet little voice within me says, "enjoy this moment." remembering I made that promise to listen. I then made my bed with a smile on my face, taking the time to make it with perfection as I fluff up my pillows and placed my teddy bear in the middle. I took a step back; I looked at my bed and really started to notice how lovely it looked with a soft blue dream catcher with a white background. Of course, I noticed my new bedding before, which was why I bought it, because it looked nice, but it was more than just the way it looked. I noticed more details that I didn't see before, like different colours of Blues intertwined with each other, Embroidered together, the little silver balls at the end of the dream catcher with feathers on each ended. I took another deep breath and said to myself, "I feel great today."

I looked in my wardrobe and I mindfully chose some clothes. I asked my body, "what colour clothes would you like to wear today?" "Orange" said my intuition. I took my clothes into the bathroom to get ready, and I looked in the mirror and I said" this moment is all I have, as yesterday is gone and tomorrow hasn't arrived. I took the moment, and I cherished it like there was no tomorrow. I wanted to get creative with my words as I had my morning wash, I told my body that I would love it and taken care of and give it what it needs. I then smiled and felt the energy within my heart chakra like a wave of pure love, wash over me. I then cleaned my teeth, taking the time to clean every Nook and cranny, I say that I don't clean properly, I do, but I rush most often to get to my next task, but today, I took my time to enjoy every moment. I smiled in the mirror and noticed my clean teeth. I got myself dressed and ready for a workout, Qi Gong, although time was catching on, I promised myself I would work out every day and started to feel reel enjoyment in the small things, instead of it feeling like a chore that I couldn't wait to be over and done with, it felt good. Then the voice says" feel the moment, enjoy the moment." I took a deep breath, and I said" I would love this workout" I chose a dance routine, Called Groovy Dance, pretty simple to follow. As I danced to the music, there was a part where you reach your arms out to the universe while sticking your chest out and you say the words, "love sets me free." One of the lyrics to the song that I was dancing to. I felt an emotional tear welling up from my eyes, but it was an emotion of pure love and happiness. I continued the session as i stood in my body for a second. I took another deep breath as I connected to my body

    Then, it was time for a quick Qigong practice to ground my energy, while I light an incense stick and switch my salt lamps on to cleanse my space. I could feel the energies around my room, peaceful, calm, inviting energies. This made me want to relax in my living room for the night and fall asleep. My energy has been off lately, that i had been resorted to my bedroom, usually happens during winter months, which is good as I often hibernate in this season and I do I love the energy and colours in my bedroom. Everything is ready for my Qi Gong practice. Just a quick 10 minutes was enough to center my energy.

    "What to do next," I asked.

    I would often make my decisions without even taking a moment to ask my heart what to do next. I guess they call this autopilot. I took some more deep breaths and looked at my old antique wooden chair under the window that I call my reading chair, although I never got the chance to read on it, as it was stuck there for show. In fact, I once placed it into the shed because there was no room in my house for it. I saw it outside a charity shop for 20 pounds. I had to buy it as it was beautiful and well worth the money. It is engraved with beautiful markings and symbols, Kind of reminds me of a chair you would find in a castle in the medieval times. That's the energy I feel from it.

I couldn't bear to see it in the shed any longer; it's too good to be hidden, so, it fetched it out and made room for it just under my window with a little Wicker footstool. My intuition spoke to me as I looked at the chair, I heard the words "read the never-ending story in the chair" At this point, I was thinking, "I have got to write as I have a deadline and I need to hoover up and wash the parts, my mind, yet again, thinking of other things to do. My inner voice speaks to me loudly," Give yourself one hour to read, Enjoy the moment. So, I made myself a cup of Chai tea and sat down on my beautiful chair, I took a moment to feel the wood to notice the carvings. I took a deep breath, and I smiled, and I said" I love this chair so much". I looked out of the window for a moment and noticed the wind was blowing and the kids were playing in the park. I felt at peace, calm, happy and in love with the flow. I didn't know where the flow was taking me, all i knew was i had to trust in the process.

I held my cup of herbal tea and felt the warmth beneath my hands, smelling the aroma of every sip, really tasting the flavors and taking notice of the detail on my cup.

I opened my book and started to read, as I read, floods of inspiring words flowed through me that I couldn't keep up with. I grabbed my book and my pen and wrote the inspiring words down for a book I had been working on. The book had come to a standstill as it needed more words to fill it up as the word count was too short. While that book had been on the back burner, I had been inspired to write another book, so I got cracking on that one. I see now how i tend to flit from one book to another with all the half-finished books. I often say to myself that I just want to work on one book at a time, as I've been writing books now for six years and haven't got one single book published yet. But the way things are going, I may have five books published in one year. Living consciously seems to have its perks.

Anyway, where was I? Oh yes, reading, of course, as I read some more, I got inspired with some more creative words. Then I was rudely interrupted by my inner voice again, which said "movie night downstairs tonight with candle-lit fairy lights on, time for a change of scenery, oh, and don't forget the plug extension for your waterfall ornament, Salt lamps and purifiers. So off I went to the town to buy an extension. When I left the house, I call upon my spirit guys to protect me and heal me, if necessary, on the journey .and I visualize a protective bubble. Being an empath can be draining, besides. I did not want to bring any unwanted negative energies into my nice, negative, energy-free home after I had cleansed it.

I set off to the shop, listening to the inner voice." Focus on this moment only. I look around me, and the feeling of peace and calm washing over me. It is a little windy but not too cold and not too hot, just right, with a little cool breeze, I closed my eyes and again, took a deep breath and breathed in the serenity. The wind gently blowing through my hair and over my face. There was a time when I would. I would get so frustrated with the wind blowing my hair and irritating me, and I would walk fast just to get to my next destination, but I had no plans to rush. I just wanted to take my time and enjoy every moment that was presented with me.

People would walk by me, complaining about the wind. Of course, I was one of those people once upon a time. I just smiled and said I love it. I got the look as if to say what a crazy lady, but I did not car, I felt happy. I stopped by a tree and said" hi, fella" I could feel he had a lot of masculine energy as I placed my hands over his bark and said, "I hope you're OK". Seemed out of character for me but they are living, breathing beings, to and deserve respect, besides, it felt good. I continued to walk through the park. It's a good thing where I live, as it's 90% trees everywhere you go, including on the pavements. I often walk through the park, but never really notice it in such depth, not like i did today. I lean up against giant stone and rest against it for a while, as the wind blew, I could smell the freshness in the air.

    I have in the past tried to practice mindfulness and being in the present moment, but I would soon get carried away with my thoughts again, but today, my intuition was so loud it overpowered my thought process, or should i say my ego. I know I've done lots of inner work and healing for the past six years and I have learnt so much about myself. I don't know what makes today any different from the other days that I practice mindfulness; The difference was the mantras that I set for myself this morning, the intention I placed upon myself.

The power of words has always been my go-to source of wisdom. On my journey and today my words have had that powerful impact.

I spotted a tiny black bird with a little orange beak. While on my walks. Hopping around the trees, I look at him Aad it looked at me, as if to say" whoops, I didn't see you there, sorry" and just hopped around back and forth as though I we both could understand each other. I just smiled, and my heart filled up with love. Under the overdrive of cuteness. Beautiful!

As I left the park to walk into town, I was called into a charity shop. I don't know why, because I only took a small amount of change with me, enough to buy my extension lead, I went in anyway and to my surprise, there was one of those ceramic money boxes that you smash with a hammer when full. I have been manifesting one of those for a few weeks because they are quite expensive to buy. Plus, I didn't want to smash it after I bought it, as they look so cute. It was still in the box for £3, so I bought it. I always call these little manifestations gifts from the universe, so I thank the universe, and I had just enough money for my extension lead. I walk back through the park coming home, as I was mesmerized by all the beauty as though I had opened my eyes for the first time. Yes, I had my spiritual awakening six years ago, and they say you literally wake from amnesia, I guess this was a second awakening.

There was something different about the street and the way they looked that I couldn't quite put my finger on. I started feeling a heightened sense of gratefulness wash over me for this beautiful moment. I was feeling grateful for the people who swept the floors of the park and for those that look after the trees, the council people who maintain the park gardens, that I would normally take for granted. The words I would describe today would be bliss, beautiful with lots of inner-love and happiness, peace and calm, grateful, magical, and optimistic. The list just goes on.

I went to the house and took a moment to appreciate the money Box I bought, as I held it in my hands, noticing the detail of the artwork. Again, I got a little distracted by my son, usually, I get a little stressed around him, as being an empath, I pick up that energy, so I went back onto autopilot and got cracking on making dinner, and I chose a salad. I was cooking, when the inner voice brings me back to the present moment again and said, "Can you hold your energy?" I knew what that meant. It means to stay in your own peaceful energy that you have created for yourself and not let energy outside yourself ruin it. I did just, I maintain my inner peace while talking to my son calmly.

I sat down on my favorite chair with my salad, and something felt odd because I was so distracted by my son's energy for a short while. I had forgotten to ask my body what it wanted to eat. I was on autopilot for that short moment; I couldn't eat my dinner. I have noticed a pattern in the past when it comes to eating. It seems that every so often, my body wants to fast and often, this is around the full moon and the new moon, But because I was previously on autopilot, I was eating for the sake of it and failed to see and feel the signs my body was telling me, so I continue to eat anyway. Then I wondered why my hiatus hernia plays up.

We follow a particular set of rules. We must eat three meals a day, breakfast, dinner and tea. So, we eat because of a pattern, or we have been told to eat that, but our bodies don't always want to eat like that, so we dismiss what it says. Then we wonder why we have problems. I put my salad in the fridge for now. It may be that my body is just not ready for it, water is what it craves. I asked my body if it wanted herbal tea and an apple, again, I took the time to smell the aroma and taste every bit, drinking the tea mindfully, and who would have known that an herbal tea could taste so nice, Sure, I like herbal teas, but I made this decision in my head to cut out traditional teas and coffees and replace with herbal teas instead, as it made sense because it wasn't a healthier option. The head isn't always wrong, and besides, the head and the heart need to work together in harmony with one another. Instead of herbal teas tasting nice for the health benefits, they taste extremely good for the taste, smell and warmth.

   Now, we get into the chores that I was originally fretting about. As I washed my sink bowl, ready to wash the pots, I looked out of the window and noticed the clouds. They were dark grey with a bright silver lining, and I love that about the clouds, normally, I would see it as a miserable day with just grey clouds. Our perception changes in the way we look at things when we are in the here and now.

   Who knew how washing pots could feel so good? it no longer feels like a chore, but instead, it feels like a good job. Each pot I cleaned i noticed how it shone, how clean they looked and smelled, every so often. Taking a deep breath as I relaxed into the cleaning. No rush for the next job. I felt pure relaxation and comfort in knowing I didn't rush the parts to get to the next task. Nothing about today felt like a chore.

I learned inspiration from today's experience and started to write more words for my book. I often keep journals and write everything down as it's part of my inner growth. Today taught me so much.

Before I know it, a title appeared on my page. Called "Conscious Living" today, Friday 21st of the 2nd 25. (Notice the Angel number 222.) Conscious Living was born. Just like my other books. When I'm in the present moment, opportunities and inspiration heighten, and Creativity is on the rise. I always know when my books are meant to be as they just flow to me in the present moment, how else can we inspiration if we not paying attention?

I have learnt to trust in the universe and that everything happens for a reason. The night is still young, 7:45 PM, and so far, I've gotten a lot done, considering I took a step back and went with the flow instead of trying to control the outcome. I lit my candles and set up my singing bowls and tuning forks for a sound healing session. I put on some nature music and sat on a cushion, mindfully sipping another cup of tea. The atmosphere was calm and soothing, and I enjoyed a good hour of relaxation.

In the past, it was so hard for me to just do this, as I got bored easily sitting and doing nothing. It is not an easy task, doing nothing, yes, a task for me. Some would call this an ADHD brain. Maybe so. It took the biggest part of six years to get to that point and i made it. To get to that point, you must learn to enjoy the moment, learn to enjoy whatever it is you're doing at the time. It's not easy to make your brain enjoy something that you don't want to do, or you find boring. The secret is to find the beauty.

who would ever think that washing the pots and doing household chores could be something enjoyable?

I watched my film as planned with my candle, late-night fluffy PJS and slippers and a nice hot chocolate. My day was nothing fancy or exciting, just a normal, what I would say, boring day, turned out to be one of the best days of my life. And that is all down to the magic of the present moment. A reason behind everything

As you go along your spiritual journey, you realise that everything that has happened in your past has happened for a reason and has shaped you into who you are today. It's as though your whole life has been one big jigsaw puzzle, and as you go along, you find a piece at a time. You come to realise that the breadcrumbs have been left for your whole life and that the messages have been there all this time, but you have been so stuck in your head to notice.

Every single person who entered my life teched me something. My abusive partner taught me to love myself. Those who used me taught me boundaries and self-respect. The abuse I suffered taught me how to forgive and to be compassionate to others. Some taught me how to love life and not take one moment of it for granted.

I thank every single person who entered my life, for I wouldn't be the beautiful soul I am today without those people. The meaning of life

Further, along your journey and the more inner work you do, you will reach higher levels of consciousness. Most people operate in what is called 3D, meaning three dimensions. Once you have an awakening, you start to step out of 3d and into 4D and 5D. These are not physical destinations; they are levels of consciousness. People who operate in 3d are operating from a place of low vibration, like complaining, gossip, anger, greed, control, hate, negativity, and illness. At the same time, those operating in higher consciousness are operating from love, compassion, happiness, joy, laughter and positivity.

The more you go into higher consciousness you go, the more you start to notice the shifts taking place, the shedding of the old you. They start off subtly and then become noticeable.

Most humans are operating from 2 levels, one of which is the victim mode; they believe that life is happening to them. The next level is the controlling stage; this was me when I just came out of victim mode, I was trying to control life. The problem with society today is that people stay in the control stage or the victim stage. As you continue inner work, you reach a level where life happens in you; you start to take a step back and listen to life instead of experiencing life. You start to think about it. The healing you have always longed for comes when you go within yourself and pay attention to your inner world and not the outer world.

When you reach a level where life happens for you, you start to get curious about what is happening rather than trying to control life or react to it. You want to understand it.

Life is not a random series of events. Instead, it's a highly intelligent event that is unfolding at just the right time, putting you exactly where you are meant to be to see and release you from the illusion that keeps you separate from the flow.

Eventually, you come to realise that life happens through you; life is always speaking to you through music, spoken words, quotes, and even pictures in the clouds, also known as synchronicities, that I spoke about earlier. You can trust life, although at times you may not like it, but even the bad stuff that happens in your life is showing you something. It knows what it's doing, but rather than struggle with it, you are open to it.

Life is beautiful

Life is a gift

Life is amazing

Life is you

And the soul says

Rest my dear

So, you can rise

Cradle your sorrows

Let tears cry from your eyes

Rest my love

Let the weight of the world crumble away

Hold yourself

Everything will be ok

Rest my child

So, you can rise

Soon, you will move to maintain

Soon, you will fly

Remember to rest

Remember the gatherings of the storm

The stillness before growth

Before the shout

That shakes your very world.

Michelle Marriott

CHOICES

I choose to be fearless.

I choose to be brave.

I choose my peace

And for that, I crave.

I choose to move forward.

I choose to leave the past.

I choose to live in the present moment

As time goes so fast

I choose to be helpful

I choose my worth

I choose to help others

For it's my purpose on earth

I choose my light

I choose my spark

I choose to be unafraid

Of the beautiful dark

I choose to learn

I choose my wealth

I choose to be creative

And be my authentic self

Michelle Marriott

About The Author

Michelle is a single parent with four children, she spent most of her life as a single parent and during that time, she loved to learn new things. Her purpose in life is to help people on their spiritual journey. She started her spiritual awakening back at the beginning of 2020, which led her to inner healing after many years of depression caused from trauma and abuse. Michelle discovered her gifts and talents, which led her down the path to Reiki and life coaching. Michelle has always been a writer, even in her younger years, and had a huge passion for it. Her dreams have always been to write and publish books.

Michelle has 5 years of experience in herbalism and natural medicine; she is a Reiki practitioner, soon to be a Reiki master. She is also trained in life coaching and holds certificates in psychology and counselling at an advanced level. She has created courses on manifestation and owns a little crafting business where she makes handcrafted gemstone jewellery and journals.

Michelle loves to play guitar, draw, write, cook, play music, bookbinding, read, craft, walk in nature, pretty much anything creative.

Book recommendations

Surrender experiment by Michael, A singer

Living Untethered by Michael, A singer

Untethered Soul by Michael A Singer

The power of now by Eckhart Tolle

A New Earth by Eckhart Tolle

The Celestine Prophecy by James Redfield

The Celestine Vision by James Redfield

The tenth insight by James Redfield

F**k it by John C. Parkins

The mastery of love by Don Miguel Ruiz

The voice of knowledge by don Miguel Ruiz

The Four Agreements by Don Miguel Ruiz

Living in the Heart by Drunvalo Melchizedek